Belarusian Theatre and the 2020 Pro-Democracy Protests

Belarusian Theatre and the 2020 Pro-Democracy Protests

Documenting the Resistance

Valleri J. Robinson

ANTHEM PRESS

Anthem Press
An imprint of Wimbledon Publishing Company
www.anthempress.com

This edition first published in UK and USA 2024
by ANTHEM PRESS
75–76 Blackfriars Road, London SE1 8HA, UK
or PO Box 9779, London SW19 7ZG, UK
and
244 Madison Ave #116, New York, NY 10016, USA

British Library Cataloguing-in-Publication Data
A catalogue record for this book is available from the British Library.

Library of Congress Cataloging-in-Publication Data
A catalog record for this book has been requested.
2023950489

ISBN-13: 978-1-83998-795-3 (Pbk)
ISBN-10: 1-83998-795-2 (Pbk)

Cover Image: Kupalaucy *Woyzeck* production photograph

This title is also available as an e-book.

CONTENTS

LIST OF FIGURES

ACKNOWLEDGMENTS

This project is first and foremost a result of John Freedman's September 2020 Facebook post introducing Andrei Kureichik and his play *Insulted. Belarus*. The Worldwide Reading Series that resulted from John's English translation and partnership with Andrei brought the events in Belarus and the theatrical response to my attention. John and Andrei galvanized an international community of theatre artists to resist authoritarianism across the globe.

In 2022, Andrei Kureichik came to the University of Illinois, Urbana-Champaign, as George A. Miller Visiting Artist at my invitation and with the support of the George A. Miller committee, Center for Advanced Studies, the Russian, East European, Eurasian Center, the European Union Center, the Department of Slavic Languages and Literatures, Krannert Art Museum, the Department of Dance, and the Department of Theatre. For eight weeks, with the support of many colleagues across the UIUC campus, Andrei and I developed several new film and theatre productions and presented lectures and film screenings in Urbana and at the University of Chicago. Artists, scholars, students, and audiences involved in the projects repeatedly told me how these events had a powerful impact on them. With Andrei, I saw firsthand the affective power of documentary theatre.

So many Belarusian artists generously talked with me and provided me with documents, interviews, and photographs. Here, I especially thank film director Aliaksei Paluyan, Vladimir Shcherban, Christina Drobysh, and other members of the Kupalautsy troupe, who helped me understand their experiences. I greatly thank Zhanna Charniauskaya, president of the Belarusians of Chicago, who made the first screening of Paluyan's film *Courage* in Chicago possible, and who has continued to support this project. I extend my thanks to Belarusian scholars, audience members, and emigres who spoke with me about their country. Additionally, I thank the theatre artists from other countries such as Siarhei Pavliuk, Javor Gardev, Olga Mysina, Igor Golyak, Bryan Brown, Jerry Adesewo, and others who shared their experiences working on Kureichik's *Insulted. Belarus*.

I wish to express my gratitude to my many colleagues and students at the University of Illinois, Urbana-Champaign, who worked on our digital reading of *Insulted. Belarus.* and our live and filmed performances of *Voices of the New Belarus.* Your rigorous engagement, curiosity, and impact on viewers strengthened my understanding of the power of these works. I give special thanks to the graduate students in my Documentary Theatre seminars, who helped develop and promote these vital works across our campus: Vincent Carlson, Emily Goodell, Dan Kipp, Laura Coby, M. Landon, Mitchel Civello, Toyosi Tejumade-Morgan, and Anne Kolaczkowski-Magee. I also greatly value the interest and encouragement of my colleagues Sandra Ruiz and Kevin Hamilton.

Finally, I thank my daughters Grace and Izzy Hohman, who joined me at screenings and performances with great interest and compassion, helped welcome a community that formed around this work in 2022, and assisted me in the final stages of completing the book.

INTRODUCTION

[...] they were the ones who could best do the only thing left to do: preserve the face of violence for the distant future.[1]

        Milan Kundera, *The Unbearable Lightness of Being*, 1984

Is this not a form of deliberate exposure and persistence, the embodied demand for a livable life that shows us the simultaneity of being precarious and acting?[2]

        Judith Butler, *Notes Toward a Performative Theory of Assembly*, 2015

On August 9, 2020, Belarus held a presidential election. The outcome was predetermined, as usual in the post-Soviet country where Aliaksandr Lukashenka held power since being elected to the presidency in 1994.[3] Over time, Lukashenka had slowly increased and concentrated power in the presidency and assured he would remain uncontested by controlling the information space and eliminating opposition.[4] In 2020, Lukashenka detained or forced major political rivals into exile prior to the election. His administration oversaw the election commission and vote counting.

---

1 Milan Kundera, *The Unbearable Lightness of Being*, New York: Harper and Row Publishers, Inc., 1984: 67.

2 Judith Butler, *Notes Toward a Performative Theory of Assembly*, Cambridge, MA and London: Harvard University Press, 2015: 153.

3 The 1994 election is generally thought to have been free and fair. Lukashenka, a regional state farm director and long-time political instructor and collective farm leader during the Soviet era, was elected in a run-off election on July 10, 1994, believed to be the last fair election. "U.S. Relations with Belarus," U.S. Department of State Bilateral Relations Fact Sheet, August 30, 2021, https://www.state.gov/u-s-relations-with-belarus/.

4 Natalia Forrat, Alyena Batura, Natallia H., and Laura Adams, "Civic Mobilization in Belarus: The Case of the 2020 Elections," Freedom House, Case Study Report (2022): 1–40, 7; "U.S. Relations with Belarus," U.S. Department of State Bilateral Relations Fact Sheet, August 30, 2021, https://www.state.gov/u-s-relations-with-belarus/.

In the evening of election day, the commission announced that Lukashenka had received 80.1% of the vote.[5] This was not surprising. This is how the four elections between 1994 and 2020 had gone, and why Belarusians were often cynical about the potential for change. What was surprising was the mass mobilization of the opposition—the largest in the 26 years of Lukashenka's rule—and the size and duration of peaceful protests that followed the election.[6]

The regime "responded with unjustified, disproportionate, and often arbitrary force."[7] For a time, this display of brute force by the State further encouraged the resistance and destabilized the notion that Lukashenka had the support of the majority of Belarusians. Eventually, with the aid of Russian authorities, dissent was suppressed through thousands of detentions and the use of torture; the closure of all independent media, arts venues, and independent nongovernmental organizations; show trials; propaganda; firings; and forced exile. Nevertheless, as Alyena Batura has written, the 2020 civic mobilization "transformed an apathetic populace into active citizens" and "led to the creation of networks of solidarity and mutual support."[8] This book looks at how several theatre artists and filmmakers joined the opposition and used their own precarious bodies and artforms to help mobilize communities, oppose the State's propaganda narratives, agitate for political prisoners, collectively mourn, and "preserve the face of violence for the distant future."

A number of developments shaped Belarusian sizable participation in the campaign rallies, elections, and protests in 2020 as distinctive from previous presidential elections since 1994. The government's dismissive attitude toward COVID-19 played a key role. With Lukashenka's refusal to impose a lockdown or enact a public health response early in the pandemic, citizens united independently through organizations like ByCovid19,

---

5 Lukashenka continues to claim this number, in spite of widespread domestic and international challenges. See the official website of the "President of the Republic of Belarus," for example, https://president.gov.by/en/president/biography; see also, Steve Rosenberg, "Belarus's Lukashenko Tells BBC: We May Have Helped Migrants into the EU," Rosenberg's interview with Lukashenka, November 19, 2021, https://www.bbc.com/news/world-europe-59343815.

6 Alyena Batura, "How to Compete in Unfair Elections," *Journal of Democracy* 33 no. 4 (Oct 2022): 47–61.

7 Anaïs Marin, "Report of the Special Rapporteur on the situation of human rights in Belarus," UN General Assembly, Human Rights Council, A/HRC/47/49/Agenda Item 4, "Human rights situations that require the Council's attention."

8 Batura, 48.

a crowdsourcing campaign to raise funds for medical equipment and encourage social distancing.[9] The expansive use of social media and the internet used by groups like ByCovid19 to coordinate in early 2020 had been fostering communities critical of government policies and developing a sense of individual responsibility for years leading up to the election.[10] Consumption of independent media on YouTube and Telegram and other platforms increased, and the audience for state-controlled TV had been gradually declining and aging in recent years.[11] For example, the independent media organization NEXTA had 49,000 subscribers on their Telegram channel in 2019 and over 1.8 million in 2021, before the government unlawfully detained its editors and writers, accusing them of extremism. It was through his YouTube channel, "A Country for Life," that Siarhei Tsikhanouski, who intended to oppose Lukashenka in the presidential elections, amassed a civically engaged audience. He used humor and a down-to-earth appearance and speech to draw out ordinary Belarusians' dissatisfaction and frustrations with the regime in 2019, and his audience steadily grew to 245,000 subscribers prior to the election.[12] After the regime arrested Tsikhanouski and rejected his candidacy for president, his wife Sviatlana Tsikhanouskaya stepped into his place.

Another popular opposition candidate, the businessman Viktar Babaryka, former head of Belgazprombank and major donor to cultural events, had a similarly large following on Facebook, and collected 435,000 signatures to support his registration to participate in the presidential election, four times the requirement to stand in an election.[13] Signature-gathering events enabled grassroots organizing and voter education.[14] Babaryka used his social media and campaign websites to publish his "Declaration for a Fair Election," that inspired civic investment in election transparency

---

9 Kata Karath, "Covid-19: How Does Belarus Have One of the Lowest Death Rates in Europe?" *BMJ* 370 (Sep 2020) https://www.bmj.com/content/370/bmj.m3543; Batura, 49.

10 Svetlana S. Bodrunova, "Social Media and Political Dissent in Russia and Belarus: An Introduction to the Special Issue. *Social Media and Society* (Oct–Dec 2021): 1–8.

11 Oleg Manaev, Natalie Rice, and Maureen Taylor, "The Evolution and Influence of Russian and Belarusian Propaganda during the Belarus Presidential Election and Ensuing Protest in 2020," *Canadian Slavonic Papers*, 63 nos. 3–4 (2021): 371–402, 374.

12 Batura, 51; Andrew Wilson, "An election in Belarus: how the west could support a marginalized opposition," European Council on Foreign Relations, July 21, 2020, https://ecfr.eu/article/commentary_an_election_in_belarus_how_the_west_could_support_a_marginalised/.

13 Wilson.

14 Natalia Forrat et al., 11.

and fairness.[15] A third potential opposition candidate, Valery Tsapkala, a former diplomat and IT entrepreneur, also used social media and signature gathering to build a popular base. However, by July 14, 2020, the government had denied Tsikhanouski, Babaryka, and Tsapkala the right to register to run. Tsikhanouski and Babaryka had been jailed, and Tsapkala soon fled the country.

The opposition then unified under Sviatlana Tsikhanouskaya, a political novice and former English teacher, whom Lukashenka viewed more as a joke than a threat.[16] Babaryka's popular campaign manager, Maryia Kalesnikava, and Tsapkala's wife Veranika joined forces with Tsikhanouskaya, running on a platform that insisted on a free and transparent election process and the promise to hold a new presidential election and release political prisoners. The three women traveled around the country holding campaign meetings and rallies in large and small cities and villages to surprising numbers of attendees. Between July 19 and July 30, their rallies in Minsk, with a population of just over two million, grew in size from 7,500 to 63,000 participants.[17] They emphasized love, hope, and unity in energizing and entertaining stage performances. Their campaign reinvigorated the symbolism of the historical white–red–white flag of Belarusian independence[18] and encouraged wearing white bracelets, representing honesty, to the polls to enable independent vote counting. Each of the three women also had a signature gesture that captured the essence of the campaign: Kalesnikava formed a heart with her hands,

---

15 Ibid., 12.

16 See, for example, Christiane Amanpour's September 8, 2020, interview with Tsikhanouskaya, "Svetlana Tikhanovskaya on the Fight Against Authoritarianism," https://www.pbs.org/video/svetlana-tikhanovskaya-fight-against-authoritarianism-jctxwx/. According to Veranika Tsapkala, Lukashenka referred openly to Tsikhanouskaya, Kalesnikava, and herself in degrading, misogynistic language. Veranika Tsapkala, Nelly Bekus, Maryna Maskaliova, and David R. Marples, "The Campaign of the 'Fighting Women': The Belarus Election of 2020 and Its Aftermath—A Conversation with Veranika Tsapkala," *Canadian Slavonic Papers*, 63 nos. 3–4 (2021): 403–421, 406.

17 Natalia Forrat et al., 15. According to the authors, the government obstructed the final planned rallies due to their popularity.

18 For a few months in Spring 1918, Belarus was an independent nation, known as the Belarusian People's Republic, and established the white–red–white flag as its national flag and symbol. This was again the national flag following the collapse of the Soviet Union until 1995 when Lukashenka restored a version of the Soviet-era green and red Belarusian flag. "Here's Why Protestors Are Flying a White-and-Red Flag," *Meduza*, August 14, 2020, https://meduza.io/en/feature/2020/08/14/here-s-why-are-protesters-in-belarus-are-flying-a-white-and-red-flag.

Tsikhanouskaya made a fist for power, and Tsakpala upheld two fingers in a victory sign.[19]

These symbols endured during the protests that followed the election commission's August 9 evening announcement that Lukashenka had received 80% of the vote, and Tsikhanouskaya received only 10%.

Incredulous and outraged at the blatant manipulation of the election outcome, thousands abruptly took to the streets in Belarus's major cities, in spite of laws prohibiting unapproved public assembly. While they might have believed a 53% Lukashenka/46% Tsikhanouskaya result, "everyone knew that 80% [for the incumbent] was absolute bullshit," Tsikhanouskaya has said.[20] She filed a complaint with the Central Electoral Commission, but she was detained by the police and forcefully deported to Lithuania.[21] Lukashenka's government then "shattered its own horrendous record for brutality," using excessive force, tear gas, stun grenades, and bullets, and mass detentions and torture in an effort to disperse crowds of protestors in the immediate aftermath of the election.[22] Unexpectedly, the degree of police violence, shared widely on Telegram channels, led to further outrage and participation in the protests, with numbers reaching as high as 400,000 in Minsk's Independence Square in mid-August.[23] In addition to moral outrage, the protestors seemed to lose their fear of the autocracy with such a large number calling for Lukashenka's resignation, according to political scientist Olena Nikolayenko.[24] Protests continued, in decreasing numbers and increasingly symbolic ways, through spring 2021, though the regime finally suppressed the opposition through high-profile and mass arrests and extreme prison sentences, torture, propaganda, censorship, internet outages, and forcing dissidents into exile.

Theatre workers joined the opposition in protest through strikes, participating in street protests, mobilizing communities through their art, and documenting the events and experiences of Belarusians surrounding the election. Theatre artists from independent theatre companies like

---

19 "Belarus: Symbols of the Opposition," *Moscow Times*, August 14, 2020, https://www.themoscowtimes.com/2020/08/14/belarus-symbols-of-the-opposition-a71146.

20 Olena Nikolayenko, "'I Am Tired of Being Afraid:' Emotions and Protest Participation in Belarus," *International Sociology* 37, no. 1 (2021): 78–96, 83.

21 Natalia Forrat et al., 17.

22 "Belarus: Unprecedented Crackdown; Arrests, Torture of Peaceful Protestors Follow Disputed Election," Human Rights Watch, January 13, 2021, https://www.hrw.org/news/2021/01/13/belarus-unprecedented-crackdown.

23 Nikolayenko, 84 and Natalia Forrat et al., 17.

24 Nikolayenko, 85–88.

the Belarus Free Theatre and the Contemporary Art Theatre had long expressed opposition to the State on their stages, if underground—in the first case, or metaphorically, in the second. State-sponsored theatres, however, remained silent and self-censoring due to strict regulations against political activities until Lukashenka unleashed such a brutal backlash against protestors.[25] As Andriej Moskwin has noted, from August 12 to 27, theatre artists from leading State-supported theatres around the country recorded and uploaded videos on YouTube and social media pleading against the government use of violence and demanding recounts of the votes.[26] Members of the capital's elite Yanka Kupala National Academic Theatre along with the Drama Theatre in Mahilou helped initiate this action supporting the opposition, and they were soon followed by the Minsk-based Puppet Theatre, the Republican Theatre of Belarusian Drama, the M. Gorky National Academic Theatre, and the Belarusian Army Theatre, as well as theatres in Brest, Vitebsk, Hrodna, and Maladzyechna.[27]

Most of these opponents were forced first from their stages, and then from the country. Many of them refused to remain silent, and they devised new ways to express their dissent, record their shock, raise awareness, and mobilize in new spaces and beyond Belarusian borders. This book aims to chart some of the work of these artists through the theatre, digital theatre, and film they produced during and in the immediate aftermath of the election and subsequent protests. Documentary theatre and film, in various modes, became a way for some of these artists to engage with their experiences and seek to draw international attention to the events in their countries. *Belarusian Theatre and the 2020 Pro-Democracy Protests: Documenting the Resistance* focuses on the work of playwright Andrei Kureichik, filmmaker Aliaksei Paluyan and his work with the Belarus Free Theatre, and the Kupalautsy theatre, an independent troupe that left the Yanka Kupala National Theatre in August 2020. An examination of their plays, films, and performances in the year after the election demonstrates the ways that theatrical performance can both represent a precarious population and embody resistance itself.

---

25 Andrei Kureichik, trans. John Freedman, "Theatre in Belarus: We Will Never Be the Same," *American Theatre Magazine*, Aug 24, 2020, https://www.americantheatre.org/2020/08/24/theatre-in-belarus-we-will-never-be-the-same/.

26 Andriej Moskwin, "Cultural Protest in Belarus: Theatres during the Belarusian Revolution (2020)," *Canadian Slavonic Papers* 63, nos. 3–4 (2021): 358–370, 362.

27 Ibid.

Documentary Theatre

If we accept Robert Leach's claim that the writer and theatre director Mikhail Pustynin developed the form of the Living Newspaper, then documentary theatre, in a sense, has its roots in Belarus.[28] Pustynin, who worked in Vitsebsk, Belarus, founded the Terevsat (Theatre of Revolutionary Satire) in 1919 to make "news" accessible to uneducated audiences in the Soviet Union through short, popular performances. Pustynin took the troupe to Moscow in 1920 and later joined the Blue Blouses, noted for performing in factories and other public spaces and popularizing the form of the living newspaper internationally. The agitprop living newspapers performed throughout Europe, the United States, and Japan in the 1920s and 1930s used live, theatrical performance to draw attention to economic and other injustices pulled from contemporary news stories in an effort to build solidarity with workers movements.[29]

Forms of documentary theatre—docudrama, tribunal plays, verbatim, witness theatre, redress theatre, and so on—have become common ways globally to address injustice, reclaim or contest representations of historical events, hold wrongdoers accountable, heal communities, build solidarity, make vulnerable populations visible, and grieve. South African playwright Athol Fugard recalled an early experience with documentary theatre at the Market Theatre in Johannesburg, where Barney Simon produced Emily Mann's *Still Life* in 1983, which "had been a great provocation to him and had revitalized his sense of theatre's role in a time of crisis."[30] Barney told Fugard that they must use the theatre to speak up and give evidence about the evils of Apartheid.[31] There is often a sense of urgency in documentary theatre because of the immediacy of the injustices represented. This sense of urgency is felt in the works represented in *Belarusian Theatre and the 2020 Pro-Democracy Protests: Documenting the Resistance*.

Documentary theatre may be built upon newspaper articles, trial transcripts, eye-witness testimonies and interviews, statistics, photographs, and film footage, but also "glances, gestures, body language, the felt experience of space, and the proximity of bodies."[32] In her edited collection, *Dramaturgy of*

28 Robert Leach, *The Revolutionary Theatre*, London and New York: Routledge, 1994: 82.
29 John W. Casson, "Living Newspaper: Theatre and Therapy," *TDR* 44, no. 2 (2000): 107–122.
30 Athol Fugard, "An Introduction," in Emily Mann, *Testimonies: Four Plays*, New York: Theatre Communications Group, 1997: x.
31 Ibid.
32 Carol Martin, ed. *Dramaturgy of the Real on the World Stage*, London: Palgrave Macmillan, 2010: 19.

the Real on the World Stage, Carol Martin notes that documentary theatre blurs the real with the represented, and unlike photography and documentary film, the "'real people' are absent—unavailable, dead, disappeared—yet reenacted."[33] Throughout this book, aspects of the real—a quote, a statistic, video footage, a felt experience—merge with the simulated, together structured and shaped by artists for both an aesthetic and a kinesthetic experience to motivate some form of political action: showing up to a solidarity march, spreading awareness, making a social media post, writing a letter to a political prisoner, or laying a flower at a grave. I examine works that firmly fall into the category of documentary theatre, such as Andrei Kureichik's verbatim *Voices of the New Belarus*; to Aliaksei Paluyan's documentary film *Courage* that captures the protests along with scenes of the documentary plays by the Belarus Free Theatre; to digital adaptations of the Kupalautsy theatre that might not be considered documentary theatre at all, if they weren't so closely linked to the felt experiences of Belarusians during the traumatizing postelection crackdown. The book aims to document the power of theatre in a time of crisis.

Judith Butler's work on precarity, precariousness, vulnerability and agency, and the performative potential of assembly have influenced my thinking about the protests in Belarus and the work of the artists represented here. These artists first placed their own bodies in extreme danger to oppose the regime as they joined in the street protests. They refused to be disposable and demanded the rights to what Butler calls a livable life, which in the Belarusian context can be understood as freedom from prison, from repression that limits free expression, from a predetermined, restrictive way of existing in the world, and, quite literally, life itself. As Butler writes, "When those deemed 'disposable' or 'ungrievable' assemble in public view … they are saying 'we have not slipped quietly into the shadow of public life: we have not become the glaring absence that structures your public life'."[34] When they could no longer appear in physical public spaces in Belarus, these artists found methods to appear otherwise—through digital forms, films, and performance spaces outside Belarus, still contesting the right to appear and to grieve those whom the State would make ungrievable. As Butler pointed out, "the streets and the square are not the only way that people assemble...."[35] The artists represented here activated the virtual spaces and theatres outside Belarus as they continued to imagine and enact a more just and democratic Belarus.

---

33 Ibid., 17.
34 Butler, 153.
35 Ibid.

The artists whose work this book features all developed in the shadow of the Nobel Prize–winning author Sviatlana Aleksievich, whose documentary novels and journalism marked her as "a dissident journalist with anti-Soviet sentiments," prior to the Soviet Union's collapse.[36] Her works such as *The Unwomanly Face of War* (1985), later staged by Anatoly Efros at the Taganka Theatre in Moscow; *The Last Witnesses: 100 Unchildlike Stories* (1985); *Zinky Boys: Soviet Voices from the Afghanistan War* (1991); later staged by Valery Raevsky at the Yanka Kupala National Theatre; and *Chernobyl Prayer* (1997) in Minsk established a polyphonic writing style that influenced a generation of Belarusians.[37] Based on interviews and testimonials, her works are assemblages that draw out multiple perspectives and viewpoints defamiliarizing traditional State narratives. Aleksievich, a member of the seven-member presidium of the Coordination Council, stood out firmly against Lukashenka and called on him to step down after the election in August 2020. Forced into exile, Aleksievich has been working to document the events related to the fraudulent 2020 Belarusian presidential election and brutal aftermath and remains a guiding light to Belarusian writers, artists, and activists living in exile.[38]

Organization of Belarusian Theatre and the 2020 Pro-Democracy Protests: Documenting the Resistance

Like documentary theatre itself, the book is organized using multi-perspectival forms of preservation. While I rely primarily on historical description and historical analysis, I also include photographs and a cornerstone interview to capture these events with multivocality and visual perspective. Photographs were selected by the artists themselves as representations of their performances and the historical events captured through the lens of the documentary. Through deep dramaturgical analysis and detail, the book chapters depict some of the essential productions of these theatre makers that capture their representation of historical events and express their traumatic experiences, while also analyzing the stylistic and aesthetic features of their work that compounded their impact. The chapters describe the way their

---

36 "Svetlana Alexievich," The Nobel Prize Website, https://www.nobelprize.org/prizes/literature/2015/alexievich/biographical/.
37 Sue Vice, "Holocaust Testimony or 'Soviet Epic': Svetlana Alexievich's Polyphonic Texts," *Holocaust Studies* 29.4 (2023): 547–565.
38 José Veraga, "On the Dangers of Greatness: A Conversation with Svetlana Alexievich," Literary Hub, June 3, 2022, https://lithub.com/on-the-dangers-of-greatness-a-conversation-with-svetlana-alexievich/.

works reached a global audience amidst the COVID-19 pandemic, raising international awareness of the crisis in Belarus while fomenting a digital age community of solidarity and collective mourning.

Chapter 1, "In Their Own Words: Andrei Kureichik's Documentary Impulse," marks the transition of popular Belarusian playwright Andrei Kureichik's work toward a radical documentary dramaturgy following the 2020 elections. The chapter offers a quick background on Kureichik's early successes before focusing on his recent plays, *Insulted. Belarus* and *Voices of the New Belarus*. In addition to the analysis of these plays as resistant archiving, the chapter examines the way a massive international community of support was cultivated and sustained by Kureichik and John Freedman, who translated both plays into English and organized the Worldwide Reading Series. Both works have been produced in dozens of countries for live stages, digital performances, and film. The chapter explores how the many productions of the two works raised awareness about the political struggles in Belarus while drawing attention to creeping authoritarianism on a global scale.

Chapter 2, "A Time for Theatre: *Courage* and the Belarus Free Theatre," focuses on the documentary film, *Courage* (2021), directed by Aliaksei Paluyan. The film subtly spotlights three actors of the underground Belarus Free Theatre in the lead-up to the 2020 election and its aftermath, blurring the domestic, theatrical, and political spaces they traversed. In addition to analyzing Paluyan's film, the chapter provides a brief historical overview of the Belarus Free Theatre and its methods of production since 2010, highlighting its use of documentary materials, physical performance style, and digital rehearsals for underground performances in Belarus. The chapter discusses strategies used by the company to build international support for resistance to Lukashenka and some of their productions depicted in Paluyan's film, drawing attention to the vitality of the theatre in times of crisis.

"An Interlude: A Documentary Interview" is the text of a conversation with the highly acclaimed, innovative Belarusian theatre director Vladimir Shcherban, based in London, whose work traverses all three book chapters. Shcherban, a director at the Yanka Kupala National Academic Theatre from 1999 to 2006, co-wrote "Manifesto for an Underground Theatre" with Andrei Kureichik while working at the national theatre.[39] Dismissed from his position at the national theatre and ultimately blacklisted, he joined

---

39 "'Nefedova byla moei luchshei podrugoi:' znamenityi rezhisser- ob ukhode iz Kupalovskogo, Svobodnom teatre I zhisni v Londone," *Zerkalo* May 30, 2023, https://news.zerkalo.io/cellar/40180.html?utm_source=twitter&utm_campaign=share&utm_medium=social&utm_content=desktop.

forces with Nicolai Khalezin and Natalia Kaliada to develop the Belarus Free Theatre and directed many of its internationally celebrated productions, including the Drama Desk nominee *Being Harold Pinter* (2011). In 2021, he appeared in Oksana Mysina's film of Kureichik's *Voices of the New Belarus*. He co-founded HUNCHTheatre, with Oliver Bennett in 2018, holding performances about politically repressed artists in London and Minsk. He offers a unique perspective on the Belarusian State and independent theatre and the potential and limits of political theatre in Belarus, past and present. Although I spoke with a number of the artists whose work is represented here, due to space limitations, I selected one critical conversation that demonstrates the many dimensions of the intersections of documentary theatre and political crises in Belarus to preserve as a singular document.

Chapter 3, "Performing Resistance Virtually: The Digital Home of the Free Kupalautsy," charts the path of a group of theatre artists who left the elite Yanka Kulpala National Academic Theatre in Minsk in solidarity with the protestors and Managing Director, Pavel Latushka, who was fired following the 2020 election. The chapter centers on the group that reformed as the free "Kupalautsy," which was banned from performing live, in their move to create digital theatre performances as acts of resistance, collective memory, and mourning. The chapter focuses on its adaptations of *Fear I, II, III* after Brecht, *Woyzeck*, and other performances that blended existing dramatic texts and the nightmarish reality of contemporary Belarus. In spite of the troupe's departure from the physical national theatre building, the free Kupalautsy claimed its identity as a national theatre, cultivating Belarusian language and culture, and continuing artistic director Mikalai Pinihin's artistic vision for a national theatre.

Belarusian Theatre and the 2020 Pro-Democracy Protests: Documenting the Resistance works to preserve a record of these theatre artists who participated in the opposition to Lukashenka through rallies on the ground, in underground spaces converted into performance venues, and through digital performance and film. While the book does not capture all who used their art as part of the resistance, it demonstrates the variety of theatrical performances that helped forge enduring entanglements and networks for change, community, and care. These artists took tremendous risks: they risked (and sometimes endured) imprisonment, exposure to violence, loss of employment and relationships, and loss of home and country. They risked their lives. This book serves as a testament to those risks and the impact of their engagement in the resistance on its durability. The communities forged through art to build solidarity, memory, and hope reveal the extraordinary power of theatre in a time of crisis.

A Note on Transliteration

Transliteration from the Belarusian and Russian generally follows the Library of Congress method without diacritical marks and is simplified for a general readership. I have adopted the preferred English spellings of émigré Belarusian artists, which has led to a number of inconsistencies and breaks with a systematic approach. Belarusians have Belarusian and Russian names, and I have opted to use the Belarusian name transliteration unless they use the Russian-based transliteration professionally. I have followed this practice for Ukrainian artists and places as well. I have maintained the romanizations used in quotations and translations; therefore, occasionally, there are multiple spellings of the same name.

Chapter 1

IN THEIR OWN WORDS: ANDREI KUREICHIK'S DOCUMENTARY IMPULSE

This text is a collective confession of a nation that has been beaten, raped, and insulted. These are the voices of the victims of violence, people who have suffered terribly. The text comprises public interviews and letters from political prisoners and Belarusians who have suffered from repression.[...] Their stories form a document. A document of historical significance.

Kureichik, Voices of the New Belarus, 2021[1]

As events were still unfolding in Belarus, playwright Andrei Kureichik turned to documentary theatre following the 2020 fraudulent election and vicious crackdown against protestors in an effort to share the story and compel an international community to press for action against Aliaksandr Lukashenka's regime. As a member of the Coordination Council created by Sviatlana Tsikhanouskaya to publicly challenge the election results and hold Lukashenka's government accountable for unlawful actions, Kureichik left Belarus when he was called before an investigative committee shortly after the election. On August 20, 2020, according to the BBC, the Prosecutor General of Belarus opened a criminal case against the Coordination Council, a representative body made up of a core group of 110 Belarusian leaders in a range of disciplines organized by Tsikhanouskaya and her team, for its efforts to "seize power" and harm national security.[2] Kureichik was advised

---

1 Andrei Kureichik, *Insulted. Belarus; Voices of the New Belarus: Two Plays of Revolution*, trans. John Freedman (n.p.: Laertes, 2003), 89.
2 Tatiana Melnichuk, "Belarus: Playwright May Be Accused of Attempting to Seize Power," August 20, 2020, *BBC News*, https://www.bbc.com/russian/features-53853205; "Rules of Procedure for the Coordination Council," Coordination Council website, updated September 6, 2020, https://rada.vision/en/rules.

to leave immediately or face indefinite imprisonment.[3] Despite what he felt were absurd allegations, he knew there was no rule of law in Belarus and left his home on August 21, 2020.[4]

In exile, still in shock from the severity of Lukashenka's violence toward the opposition, Kureichik immediately went to work using the only tools at his disposal—his playwriting skills and network of theatre workers. In September 2020, he wrote the play *Insulted. Belarus.*, which directly represents the clash between Lukashenka's regime and the pro-democracy resistance in 2020, using real names and verbatim texts along with fictional, metaphorical material that captures the feelings, as he experienced it, of the August events. The following year, Kureichik wrote the play *Voices of the New Belarus*, an entirely verbatim piece based on the real texts of real political prisoners in Belarus. Though building on verbatim accounts, Kureichik masterfully arranges the material into a dynamic piece for the theatre beyond mere reporting. The two plays are quite distinctive dramaturgically, both in terms of structure, subject, and style, yet both strategically employ authentic accounts and foreground documentation to build supportive communities, sustain hope, and collectively mourn. With English-language translator and celebrated Russian theatre critic, John Freedman, Kureichik launched the Worldwide Readings Project that had theatre artists around the world sharing the stories of the protests in Belarus and the political prisoners trapped by the regime.[5] This chapter highlights the far-reaching impact of Kureichik and Freedman's partnership and how they fortified a community of resistance.

Prior to the August 2020 Presidential elections in Belarus, Kureichik had secured international renown, particularly in Belarus, Russia, and Ukraine, for his celebrated plays and screenplays. With over 20 popular screenplays for film and television, including high-grossing films like *Above the Sky* (2013),

---

According to the Rules of Procedure, the council "does not aim to seize state power in an unconstitutional manner, nor does it call to organize and prepare actions that disrupt the public order." It acknowledges election violations and violent actions by law enforcement, denounces the election results as fraudulent, and advocates for the freedom of political prisoners.

3 Andrei Kureichik, public talk, "Performing Resistance to Authoritarianism," April 14, 2022, Tryon Festival Theatre, Krannert Center for the Performing Arts, University of Illinois, Urbana-Champaign, https://cas.illinois.edu/node/2588.

4 Tatiana Melnichuk, "Belarus: Playwright May Be Accused of Attempting to Seize Power," August 20, 2020, *BBC News*, https://www.bbc.com/russian/features-53853205.

5 See "Insulted. Belarus" website, created by Bryan Brown, for numerous documents of the Worldwide Reading Series and press. https://www.insultedbelarus.com/.

Office Romance (2011), and *Lovey Dovey* and *Lovey Dovey 2* (2007–2008), audiences throughout Eastern Europe knew the writer for his tightly plotted comedies, suspense thrillers, and detective series, such as *Odessa Mama* (2011). Although Kureichik had been educated as a lawyer, which he practiced for some time, his writing career emerged almost by surprise when he submitted a play, *Piedmont Beast*, for a competition at the Moscow Art Theatre in 2002. The play won the competition and a staging at Moscow's famous theatre that year, earning it the award for Best Contemporary Play by the Russian Ministry of Culture. Soon after, his plays were staged and won awards throughout Eastern Europe.

One of his most produced plays, *Three Giselles*, won the prize for comedy at the 2004 International "Kolyada-Plays" Theatre Festival founded and produced by Nikolai Kolyada in Yekaterinburg, Russia. The play, though billed as a comedy, reveals Kureichik's early use of genre-blurring techniques and a sly undercurrent of political critique in his pre-2020 dramatic works. In the play, Kureichik weaves together three periods of the life of a woman named Giselle. She is depicted through nonlinear scenes as a young woman in her home in France during World War II, in her rural life with an abusive husband in Belarus in 1957, and in her final days in Post-Soviet Belarus, as an isolated great-grandmother, too old to go home to France when she is finally free in 1999. The comedy of the play comes from the political platitudes of the communists in France and Belarus bumping up against the everyday reality of the working characters, typically women. Samuel Beckett's absurdism and Arthur Adamov's sense of the ridiculous in Soviet life merge in the play to create a heart-wrenching tragicomedy. Performed throughout post-Soviet Eastern Europe for a decade, the play captures the absurdity as well as the brutality and misogyny of Soviet life. It should be noted that a critique of the Soviet system also poked fun at Lukashenka's regime, as it dreamed to maintain and restore the false sense of agricultural and economic dominance during the Soviet period. What's striking about the play is the degree to which the brutality of hypermasculinity in the Soviet era is represented. In retrospect, the play seems to warn against the reemergence of the misogyny and violence that accompanies authoritarianism.

Kureichik only recently became more directly involved in opposition to Lukashenka's regime. In his lecture, "Performing Resistance to Authoritarianism," at the University of Illinois, Urbana-Champaign, in April 2022, Kureichik discussed the important role he played in Tsikhanouskaya's campaign for the presidency. Because she and her partners were political novices, they didn't have deep experience organizing the shape of political rallies, one of the strongest formats for mobilizing support in Belarus at the time. As a storyteller, Kureichik understood the importance of developing scenarios for the rallies, so he worked with the team on the structure, formatting, and messaging of the rallies. Rather than focusing on garnering emotion by demonizing and defeating the regime, he and Tsikhanouskaya's team shaped their message around building communities through trust, hope, and love. Their events were dynamic, popular performances showing the possibilities in a post-Lukashenka Belarus.

Insulted. Belarus.

Soon after fleeing Belarus, Kureichik swiftly wrote the play *Insulted. Belarus.* in an effort to capture the disorientation and shock experienced by so many Belarusians in the lead-up and brutal aftermath of the August 2020 Presidential election in Belarus. The text, originally titled *Insulted. Belarus(sia).*, is a blend of verbatim material from speeches and interviews that grounds the play in the historical moment interspersed with created dialogue to portray chaotic emotional shifts and create a clear narrative arc. Kureichik uses humor and a sense of the ridiculous as the play moves from the mundane to the grotesque to capture a nightmarish scenario reflecting the experience of many Belarusians.

The play centers on seven characters who represent various perspectives and roles in the events surrounding the elections. This includes Oldster (Aliaksandr Lukashenka), Youth (his son), Novice (Sviatlana Tsihanouskaya), Cheerful (modeled on Maryia Kalesnikava), Raptor/Avian (a Pro-Regime mercenary riot policeman), Corpse (modeled on the first victim of the regime's violence, Aliaksandr Taraikovski), and Mentor (a pro-Regime election official and teacher). The dramatic action builds through a series of monologues and a few short moments of dialogue and fragments that create jarring tonal shifts and a sense of confusion. The play begins with a series of introductory monologues that establish the seven characters' dominant traits, suggested by their archetypal names, and their perspectives on their country and the elections. Following these introductions, Raptor introduces the coming turmoil through a disjointed monologue, interrupted by a phone call from his fiancée, that anticipates the disruption of normal life. Act One ends with rapid fragments depicting the celebration of Tsikhanouskaya's win, the shutting down of the internet, the sense of shock and outrage at the revelation of fraudulent election results, Lukashenka's growing rage, and the explosion of a grenade. Structurally and rhythmically, Kureichik depicts disorientation and disillusionment in the immediate aftermath of the election.

Act Two places the characters amidst the firestorm of the postelection crackdown. Raptor abuses Cheerful and Corpse, who defiantly try to protect her; Mentor attempts to avoid the chaos to protect her pension; Novice reveals how interrogators threatened her and sent her to Lithuania, while Oldster grows increasingly ruthless. He blames the protestors and the West for the need for the violent repression. In the closing scenes of the play, as Oldster continues to rage, Mentor experiences a reversal and recognition when she realizes her daughter has been arrested. Cheerful and Novice close the play, still hopeful, in spite of the regime's terror, because of the courage they have seen among their fellow Belarusians. The protest song "Walls" by Lluis Llach plays as the drama ends.

Like many documentary plays, Kureichik's work functions on several levels. While it uses documentary texts, the play has an agitprop, rather than strictly journalistic, character that drives its shape and purpose. Even as it expresses the experience of the pro-democratic protestors, it ridicules and lambasts Lukashenka as an immoral, reactionary remnant of Soviet culture and celebrates the heroic freedom fighters. Kureichik seamlessly blends distinctive characteristics of satire, romanticism, Eastern European new drama, and tragedy into the work. His masterful dramaturgy and stylistic blending, though, captured a reality that audience members noted as authentic. After watching the online English-language premiere reading by the Los Angeles-based Rogue Machine Theatre on YouTube, one person wrote in the chat, "As a Belarusian I find this play brilliant! It resembles all the feelings we all had and gives a great picture of how it all was. A HUGE thanks for having this play in English. For those who speak English and barely understand the situation—I can tell. It is just as it was. Long Live Belarus."[6] Similarly, Belarusian audience members for the YouTube presentation of the World Premiere live performance in Kherson, Ukraine, wrote in the comments about how the play presented the truth of their experiences. "I watched the reading—I cried and now [...] I remembered everything. Truth. Much thanks."[7] One viewer applauded the performance and called the genre, "tragic satire." As evinced by the many comments on the digital platforms of over 200 performances, Kureichik's perspective on the events resonated deeply with audiences.

---

6 Rogue Machine Theatre, *Insulted. Belarus(sia).*, online performance, https://www.youtube.com/watch?v=XYf6lFRXTGQ&t=952s.

7 "Obizhennie. Belarus'(sia). Spektakl' Akademicheskogo Teatra im. M. Kypala. Postanovka Sergeya Pavlyuka." Recording of live performance, November 1, 2020, https://www.youtube.com/watch?v=2DNN9Vt54As.

Oldster first appears in the play with the words, "I hate theatre."[8] He critiques art as useless and wasteful. Rather abruptly, he becomes menacing as he describes his attraction to horses:

> They're quiet and they obey. They work until they drop.[...] Yeah, mares can be a bit feisty, but you just give her a little whack on the head, and she'll calm right down. Then put blinders on her, and you can run her into the fire or water. She's loyal [...] Like a country should be.[9]

This suggestion of violence, misogyny, and dominance becomes further articulated, and directed at the protestors, as the play progresses. In the final scene of the play, he tells his son who is carrying a machine gun, "It's easy, kid. You aim it at a person, a traitor, any traitor, you give him a good look and squeeze the trigger. Pop! The traitor's gone. It's easy, son."[10] Lukashenka has long portrayed himself as strong and dominant through images and video with weapons and in the proximity of the military or police. On August 24, 2020, he released footage of himself emerging from a helicopter outside the presidential palace carrying an assault rifle, alongside his rifle-wielding teenage son, and thanking the riot police barricading the gate.[11]

In addition to presenting the leader's hypermasculine tyrannical outlook, the character of Oldster represents "Belorussia," of the original title. Kureichik captured the fight between the country's past and future in the original Russian-language title, *Obizhennye. Belarus'(sia).*, later simplified by Freedman and Kureichik in English, due to the nuance lost in translation. The Russian word for Belarus transliterates as Belarussia, Belorussia, or Byelorussia, depending on the system, and was in use by Russians to refer to the region under the Russian Empire and was officially adopted in 1922, when Belarus joined the USSR as the Belarussian Soviet Socialist Republic. Since 1991, the country's official name is the Republic of Belarus, though many Russians and Belarusians associated with an affinity for the Soviet past or union state with Russia continue to call the country by this name. Members of the opposition emphasize the independence of Belarus and break with the past by insisting on the name Belarus.

---

8 Kureichik, *Two Plays*, 37.

9 Ibid., 37.

10 Ibid.,79.

11 Yuliya Talmazan, "Belarus Strongman Lukashenko Wears Body Armor, Carries Rifle as Protests Continue," *NBCNews*, August 24, 2020, https://www.nbcnews.com/news/world/belarus-strongman-lukashenko-wears-body-armor-carries-rifle-protests-continue-n1237820.

In the play, Lukashenka's supporters are represented through Mentor, an aging school teacher who has benefitted from the regime's corrupt political system, and Raptor, the career riot policeman who worked the 2014 Maidan protests in Ukraine and aspires to a more settled position in Russia. If Mentor, until her recognition, serves as a laughable mouthpiece of Lukashenka's propaganda, Raptor represents the base violence and misogyny that maintain the regime's power through terror. Mentor's shift from the beginning to the end, from ignorance to knowledge, is the greatest and captures the tragic dimensions of the play. Raptor, like Oldster, only hardens in his impulses. Raptor's coarseness is reminiscent of what has been called Russian New Drama, a genre that explicitly expresses raw, revolting, and violent tendencies in the absence of hope and care.[12] Hypermasculinity shapes the worlds in which the powerful prey on anyone perceived as weak. Using sexually explicit and heterosexist language, verbal and physical abuse, and degradation, Raptor clearly thrives on the authority of his position. "Observe this, cunt," he says to Cheerful, an election observer in the opening of Act II, "Shut your trap, into the prison van, cow [...]."[13] He contemplates raping her, even after he identifies her as his fiancee's sister. His hypermasculine aggression parallels his stolid antidemocratic position. In his final line, he expresses to a colleague, "Well, Renat [...] I can feel it in my bones, when we go to back Putin, we won't fuck that one up!"[14] Kureichik wrote the play a year and a half before Putin's invasion of Ukraine in February 2022, yet the character Raptor makes clear how Putin and Lukashenka's violent, antidemocratic collaborations threatened the entire region, relying on the anti-Western stance and misogynistic belligerence of the regimes and their supporters.

The final character on the regime's side in *Insulted. Belarus.* is Youth. This character represents Mikalai Lukashenka, the teenage son of Aliaksandr Lukashenka. Many speculate that Lukashenka has been grooming this third son, who often attends official international diplomatic events with his father, to become his successor.[15] In the play, Youth threatens, "If you don't turn on the internet, I'm not going to be president after you!" His father jokes

---

12 See John Freedman, *Real and Phantom Pains: An Anthology of New Russian Drama*, Washington, DC: New Academia Publishers, 2014 for an introduction and examples.

13 Kureichik, 61.

14 Ibid., 79.

15 "Protest Plagued Belarus Strongman Transfers Son to Moscow School," *The Moscow Times*, September 18, 2020, https://www.themoscowtimes.com/2020/09/17/protest-plagued-belarus-strongman-transfers-son-to-moscow-school-reports-a71474.

back to an interviewer, "He's the leader of the opposition in my house."[16] Lukashenka himself had made the claim in a public interview before the August election that his son was "inclined to oppose power in general."[17] In the play, the character of Youth serves as both comic relief as he banters with his father and to demonstrate the way the regime inculcates the young into systemically violent, antidemocratic beliefs. Carrying a machine gun in the play's conclusion, mirroring Lukashenka's real teenage son brandishing a rifle on August 24, 2020, the character Youth is no longer an innocent child.[18] His final line in the play is "Who do we shoot?"[19]

Oldster would have his son shoot "Rats [...] Prostitutes, drug addicts! Sheep! Cannon fodder!"[20] That is, anyone who opposes him. For decades, Lukashenka has characterized those who oppose him as disposables with dehumanizing language. In a truncated interview with BBC's Steve Rosenberg in November 2021, he refers to the protestors as "traitors" and accuses them of being agents of the West, which he considers the EU, UK, and US.[21] He tells Rosenberg, "We'll massacre all of the scum that you have been financing."[22] In October 2020, when the Belarusian police were authorized to use lethal weapons against the protestors, First Deputy Interior Minister Gennady Kazakevich characterized the protestors as "militants, radicals, anarchists and football hooligans."[23]

In Kureichik's play, the opposition to the regime is depicted by Novice, Cheerful, and Corpse. As Sviatlana Tsikhanouskaya early in her political and diplomatic career, Kureichik presents her as she often represented herself. A reluctant politician and mother, she took on the role of leader of the opposition and presidential candidate when her husband was denied the ability to run. In the play, she grows from an uncertain and overwhelmed woman to a resolved, unrelenting political leader. In her first monologue

---

16 Kureichik, 54.

17 "Protest Plagued Belarus Strongman Transfers Son to Moscow School," *The Moscow Times*, September 18, 2020, https://www.themoscowtimes.com/2020/09/17/protest-plagued-belarus-strongman-transfers-son-to-moscow-school-reports-a71474.

18 https://www.nbcnews.com/news/world/belarus-strongman-lukashenko-wears-body-armor-carries-rifle-protests-continue-n1237820.

19 Kureichik, 78.

20 Ibid.

21 Steve Rosenberg, "Belarus's Lukashenko Tells BBC: We May Have Helped Migrants into EU," *BBC News*, November 19, 2021, https://www.bbc.com/news/world-europe-59343815.

22 Ibid.

23 "Belarus Protests: Police Authorized to Use Lethal Weapons," October 12, 2020, *BBC News*, https://www.bbc.com/news/world-europe-54513568.

in the play, Novice talks about the best way to make patty cakes, ground beef, or pork patties with "onion, garlic, and spices." Novice emerges as a woman who has avoided direct political involvement because of the emotional exhaustion of such work. She served her husband, the popular blogger and potential presidential candidate Siarhei Tsikhanouski, his favorite foods "to get his mind off things," and turned her phone off, so the "BBC, CNN, ours and other channels harass me all the time."[24] Through the course of the play, in part due to the direct threats by interrogators who forced her to flee when she tried to lodge a complaint with the Central Elections Committee, Novice emerges as the willing spokesperson of the opposition. The narrative in the play and the one repeated in the global press maintained that she was an average woman who became involved in the movement for the love of her family and her country.[25] As a self-less, nonviolent, formerly apolitical "everyman," she was emblematic of the character of the pro-democracy movement in Belarus.

Cheerful is modeled on Maryia Kalesnikava, the classical flutist and supporter of presidential candidate Viktar Babaryka, imprisoned prior to the elections. She joined forces with Tsikhanouskaya to support her candidacy. Belarusians celebrated Kalesnikava's upbeat, positive attitude, smile, and perspective that shaped the nature of the rallies and protests. Referring to her as "the smiling activist," journalist Sarah Rainsford noted that even Tsihanouskaya fed off her "energy, enthusiasm- and bravery."[26] In the play, Cheerful is an election observer and sister to the fiancée of the Riot Policeman, Avian. At the opening of the play, she fully believes the election is fair and that Tsikhanouskaya's win will be honored. She's stunned and disoriented when false election results are presented, and she and others are brutally handled by the riot police when they protest. Even in the prison van, and later in the prison, she still finds signs of love and hope. As Kureichik writes the character, her spirit cannot be crushed. This parallels the images of Maryia Kalesnikava dancing a year later in a glass cage in court prior

---

24 Kureichik, 47.
25 Svetlana Tikhanovskaya, "I Was a Stay-at-Home Mom. Now I'm Leading a Revolution," *New York Times*, September 23, 2020, https://www.nytimes.com/2020/09/23/opinion/belarus-tikhanovskaya-opposition-leader.html; Stephanie Fillion, Tikhanovskaya: From Stay-at-Home Mom to Opposition Leader," *Forbes*, September 4, 2020; Sarah Rainsford, "Belarus, The Stay-at-Home Mum Challenging an Authoritarian President, *BBC News*, August 1, 2020, https://www.bbc.com/news/world-europe-53574014.
26 Sarah Rainsford, "Maria Kolesnikova: No Regrets for Belarus Activist Jailed for Coup Plot," *BBC News*, September 30, 2021, https://www.bbc.com/news/world-europe-58719084.

to the announcement of her 11-year prison sentence for conspiracy to seize power, threatening national security, and other charges.[27] In spite of ongoing evidence of ill-treatment in prison, she forcefully and defiantly remained optimistic as a signal to her supporters to stay firm in their resolve when she had opportunities before a camera.

In Kureichik's play, the character Corpse is an amalgamation of protestors, but largely an embodiment of Aliaksandr Taraikouski, the first victim of the regime's crackdown on the 2020 protests who was shot and killed in the protests on August 10, 2020. The Belarusian police claimed Taraikouski killed himself when an explosive device detonated in his hand, but video footage shows he was shot in the chest and empty-handed and his partner, Elena German, contested the government's claims.[28] In the play, Kureichik imagines him in the prison van, heroically trying to protect Cheerful. Even as he dies, he sings the protest song, "Destroy the Prison Walls," popularized in Belarus in the 2020 election protests. The song is a Belarusian adaptation of Jacek Kaczmarski's 1968 Polish Solidarity song, "Mury."[29] As Tsikhanouskaya's senior political advisor Frank Viacorka posted on his Twitter account, recognizing how the Polish movement inspired the Belarusians, the main lines of the song are as follows: "Pull the teeth of the prison bars from the walls! Tear off the chains, break the whip, and the walls will fall, will fall, will fall, and will bury the old world."[30] Kureichik, still processing the recent events in which he participated and deeply felt the impact of the collective singing, ends the play with the song.

After writing the play, Kureichik sent it to John Freedman, the celebrated theatre critic formerly with the *Moscow Times*, author, and translator, to see if he would translate the play and help generate interest in having the play performed internationally.[31] Neither Kureichik nor Freedman anticipated the astonishing response by theatre makers around the globe.[32] Dozens of

---

27 Paraic O'Brien, "Belarus Opposition Leader Maria Kalesnikava Jailed," *Channel 4 News*, UK, September 6, 2021, https://www.channel4.com/news/belarus-opposition-leader-maria-kalesnikava-jailed.

28 "'Shot Right in the Chest:' Partner Denies Belarus Protestor Died from Own Bomb," *The Guardian*, August 16, 2020, https://www.theguardian.com/world/2020/aug/16/shot-right-in-the-chest-partner-denies-belarus-protester-was-killed-by-own-bomb.

29 Paula Erizanau, "How One Song Became the Anthem of the Pro-Democracy Protests in Belarus," New East Digital Archive, July 27, 2020, https://www.calvertjournal.com/articles/show/12004/belarus-pro-democracy-protests-song-anthem.

30 https://twitter.com/franakviacorka/status/1288929550043361280.

31 Bryan Brown, "The Translation of Protest: The Worldwide Readings Project of Andrei Kureichyk's *Insulted. Belarus.*" *New Theatre Quarterly* (2023): 1–17.

32 Ibid., 1.

theatre organizations, professional and academic, expressed immediate interest. Freedman translated the play quickly into English, editing continuously as early digital readings were presented, and the Worldwide Readings Project took shape.[33] Many theatre workers around the world were in lockdown mode, due to COVID-19. Theatres were closed, and film projects had been cancelled. Meanwhile, amidst the pandemic, right-wing would-be autocrats seemed to be gaining momentum and attempting to suppress democracy globally. A Freedom House report noted, "As a lethal pandemic, economic and physical insecurity, and violent conflict ravaged the world in 2020, democracy's defenders sustained heavy new losses in their struggle against authoritarian foes, shifting the international balance in favor of tyranny."[34] Global democratic decline and the increasing use of surveillance, police brutality, and force against dissidents primed the reception of Kureichik's play.

When Freedman reached out to the many theatre workers in his network, they replied with resounding enthusiasm to engage with Kureichik's resonant work.[35] Early readings, such as the English-language digital premiere by Rogue Machine Theatre on September 18, 2020, directed by Guillermo Cienfuegos focused on raising awareness of the crisis in Belarus. Readings took place on Zoom, Facebook, and YouTube platforms, with many talkbacks with Kureichik and Freedman. One especially committed company, Arlekin Players Theatre, under the direction of Igor Golyak, offered numerous professional and aesthetically nuanced readings in English and Russian. As I've written elsewhere:

> one powerful presentation by the group, Belarus-based actor Ales Malchanau joined the live performance as Corpse on October 18, 2020. Positioned before a window that looked out over Minsk, Malchanau's cinematic performance displayed the full range of his character through distilled physical action and vocal dexterity. He moved gracefully from a boisterous and energetic hockey fan to a committed freedom fighter, wrapping himself in the historical white-red-white flag of the opposition, to a still, heartbroken, and gentle wounded warrior.[36]

---

33 Irina Yakubovsky, "Raw, Revolutionary, and Painfully Honest: Insulted. Belarus(sia)" *The Theatre Times*, October 23, 2020, https://thetheatretimes.com/raw-revolutionary-and-painfully-honest-insulted-belarussia/.

34 Sarah Repucci and Amy Slipowitz, "Democracy under Siege," https://freedomhouse.org/report/freedom-world/2021/democracy-under-siege.

35 Ibid.

36 Valleri Robinson, Review of *Insulted. Belarus. Worldwide Readings*, by Andrei Kureichik. *Theatre Journal* 73, no. 3 (2021): 427–429.

The energized online chat screens and postshow discussions demonstrated that this and other performances activated audience members' empathy, curiosity, and rage.[37] Although the text focused on the events in Belarus, audiences found resonance with other global events. The project and its meaning expanded to capture the anxieties around democratic decline and the memories of independence movements in the post-Soviet sphere.

The World Premiere live stage performance took place at the Mikola Kulish Academic Theatre in Kherson, Ukraine. Directed by Siarhei Pavliuk, the production vividly drew out the satirical elements of the play. Using broad physical and vocal humor, the actors appeared from the auditorium, first representing the pro-regime characters, followed by the pro-democracy side. Each actor entered, postured in character type, and toyed with the audience and other actors on the stage. Audiences applauded as their favorite actors took the stage, even if they appeared as villains. The introductory scenes, rearranged from Kureichik's original text, were both mocking and playful. A self-satisfied Lukashenka, played by Oleksandr Liubchenko as approval-seeking and out of touch, was mocked by his son (Konstantin Rogan) and out-manipulated by Mentor, played by Svitlana Zhurvl'ova, an audience favorite, who knew just the right tone to use for her wide-ranging role. The stage was divided into two sides, marked by their representative flags and TV screens presenting either State media (Channel 1) or independent news (Nekhta). A long table in the middle connected the sides and was used ingeniously as a platform stage as the violence escalated. The production, making use of incessant audiovisual material, raucous audio, and broad physicality, was loud, garish, jarring, mocking, and seething in its solidarity with the Belarusian protestors. In the final moments of the production, the entire cast raised a huge white–red–white flag in solidarity, and the audience erupted in enthusiastic applause.

In addition to the numerous digital readings and live performances, several film versions of *Insulted. Belarus.* were made. Directorial approaches to the material varied widely, revealing a surprising range of stylistic interpretations. If Pavliuk drew out the play's potential for broad agitational satire, filmmakers Oksana Mysina and Javor Gardev found two alternative readings of the work. Both films were made using COVID-19 protocols using solo performers and limited technical support. Russian director and celebrated film and stage actress, Mysina, created a poetically naturalistic

---

37 *Insulted. Belarus(sia)*, Arlekin Players Theatre, online performance Dir. Igor Golyak, April 18, 2021, https://www.youtube.com/watch?v=r4yud4Y9G2A.

Insulted. Belarus. Dir. Siarhei Pavliuk, Photos by Mikola Kulish Theatre (Kherson, Ukraine).

film that incorporated imagistic montage and rhythmic editing and sound to capture the preelection hope and disorienting, chaotic, violent aftermath. The actors, stars of the Russian and Belarusian stages, filmed themselves in various natural interior and exterior settings and performed their roles in an understated, realistic manner. The film premiered on Russia's TV Rain Channel on November 12, 2020, before the station was shut down by the Russian government. Bulgarian stage and film director, Javor Gardev, best known for his award-winning film *Zift* (2008), created a haunting, stylized version, with a near Shakespearean scale. The effect is developed through vocally and physically assertive, sharp, crisp presentations by the actors on a minimalist gray background in which an indistinct figure appears to protrude into and surveil the prisonlike, figurative environment. Gardev's version captures the nightmarish world of Kureichik's play with a universal dimension. Most chilling in the film, and unique in its distillation of the moment, is the slight smile of Youth when his father tells him to shoot. Gardev noted this as the moment in the "son's arc of inevitably, unwillingly becoming the Dragon."[38]

The play *Insulted. Belarus.* and the Freedman and Kureichik's Worldwide Reading Project generated a remarkable and powerful network of theatre artists and scholars who found unique ways to participate

---

38 Email to the author, April 4, 2022.

Nadya Keranova as Cheerful in *Insulted. Belarus.* by Andrei Kureichik, Dir. Javor Gardev, Photography by Javor Gardev.

in the project. In addition to 30 translations, hundreds of live and digital readings, live performances, and film screenings, there were dozens of publications, numerous fundraising events, and a website (insultedbelarus. com) launched by Bryan Brown to ensure that events surrounding the 2020 Presidential election in Belarus are not forgotten. The astonishing scale of the project mobilizing international artists, which grew yet again following the start of the Russian War against Ukraine, testifies to the power and potential of art workers to work together to resist autocracy.

Voices of the New Belarus

From its outset, the opposition movement under the leadership of Sviatlana Tsikhanouskaya centered on three key items: free and fair elections, constitutional reform, and the release of political prisoners. In exile, members of the Coordination Council maintained the release of Belarusian political prisoners as a focal point of its work. Tsikhanouskaya regularly designates days of solidarity with political prisoners widely announced on social media, encouraging rallies, letter-writing campaigns, and artistic events drawing attention to the ongoing unlawful imprisonment of Belarusian politicians, journalists, human rights workers, artists, and others who criticize Lukashenka's regime. On May 20, 2023, the U.S. State Department condemned "the Lukashenka regime for unjustly holding over 1,500 political prisoners."[39] As a member of the Organization for Security and

---

39 "Over 1,500 Political Prisoners in Belarus," press statement, U.S. Department of State, May 20, 2023, https://www.state.gov/over-1500-political-prisoners-in-belarus/.

Co-operation in Europe (OSCE), Belarus has committed to human rights, free expression and media freedom, democracy and fair elections, fair trials, and other requirements for membership in the organization. In his 2021 BBC interview with Rosenberg, Lukashenka denied the existence of political prisoners in Belarus, claiming they were all traitors and agents of foreign governments, who had broken Belarusian law. In the interview, he admitted torture in Akrestsina Prison, but justified it, claiming policemen were injured as well.[40] In September 2022, U.S. Ambassador Michael R. Carpenter noted to the OSCE Permanent Council in Vienna that "Political prisoners are held in freezing, overcrowded, and filthy conditions. They are deprived of food, water, sleep, and personal hygiene. And they endure severe beatings and are denied medical care."[41] He recommended 13 items from the 1991 Moscow Mechanism of the OSCE to further human rights, democracy, and the rule of law in Belarus. Nevertheless, the number of political prisoners continues to rise in the country.

As of September 2021, when Kureichik wrote *Voices of the New Belarus*, there were nearly 1,000 political prisoners recognized by the Viasna Human Rights organization and as prisoners of conscience by Amnesty International. A few months earlier, the U.N. Special Rapporteur on the situation of human rights in Belarus, Anaïs Marin reported with alarm the number of verifiable reports of torture, rape, detention, and abuse of children, degrading treatment of prisoners, and impunity for perpetrators since the 2020 elections.[42] Marin noted the "record number of arbitrary arrests and detentions" leading up to the elections and in the immediate aftermath.[43] She made 101 recommendations for improving human rights in Belarus. Kureichik wrote *Voices of the New Belarus* to draw attention to these unlawful detentions and the show trials of the regime and to document cases of torture and abuse for international investigations.

Kureichik examined over 400 publicly available documents—letters, testimonies, newspaper editorials, and interviews in search of the ways

---

40 Steve Rosenberg, "Belarus's Lukashenko Tells BBC: We May Have Helped Migrants into EU," *BBC News*, November 19, 2021, https://www.bbc.com/news/world-europe-59343815.

41 Michael R. Carpenter, "On the sentencing of political prisoners in Belarus," remarks to OSCE Permanent Council, September 15, 2022, https://by.usembassy.gov/on-the-sentencing-of-political-prisoners-in-belarus/.

42 Anaïs Marin, "Report of the Special Rapporteur on the situation of human rights in Belarus, Anaïs Marin," May 4, 2021, A/HRC/47/49, 1–20. https://www.ohchr.org/en/documents/country-reports/ahrc4749-report-special-rapporteur-situation-human-rights-belarus-anais.

43 Ibid., 8.

the imprisoned represented their arrests, their trials, their experiences in the prisons, and their various personal responses to the violent, chaotic, bewildering legal and penitentiary system of the regime. He noted parallel stories, overlapping references to specific prison guards, detailed representations of torture and abuse, acts of kindness and solidarity, and the range of personal perspectives—from the ironic to the despondent to the hopeful—on events that led to their imprisonment. From these documents, he selected 16 accounts by Belarusians who represented a broad cross section of political prisoners, some who remain in prisons and others who have been released.[44] Kureichik selected texts from well-known political figures and activists along with less famous students, artists, IT workers, journalists, and people who just happened to be in the wrong place at the wrong time. On the balance, the text combats the representation of the activists as criminals, terrorists, and puppets controlled by Western puppeteers, which Lukashenka expressed nearly a dozen times in his aforementioned 2021 BBC interview with Steve Rosenberg.

In the original version of the play, before Kureichik added a 17th monologue featuring 2022 Nobel Peace Prize-winning activist Ales Bialiatski, it opened with text from an interview with Vitaly Marokko, a 40-year-old logistics specialist, who shared his story with the internet news database, August2020, which collected documentary evidence, including medical reports and photographs, of victims of the regime's violence.[45] In the excerpt for the play's opening, Marokko confesses that he hadn't been politically active until now but felt that the time had come to demand change. On the night of the election, he went with his son to the city center on August 9 to hear the official results of the election, but they weren't announced. Nearly 500 people had gathered and became increasingly agitated when the results weren't posted. The riot police, he says, began spraying tear gas and firing shots into the crowd. He was wounded by a stun grenade and eventually taken to the hospital. In the monologue selected for the piece, Marokko tells about the strangers who offered to help him, including a woman with a car with a white interior. "'I'll wait for an ambulance, I said.' I couldn't bear to ruin the interior of her car, the flow of blood was getting worse."[46]

44 This discussion is based on the original version of the text. Kureichik later added a monologue by the imprisoned human rights activist and 2022 Nobel Peace Prize winner, Ales Bialiatski, to the beginning of the play. There are several other variations between the unpublished manuscript used in early productions and the 2023 publication, so I will cite from the published version, when possible, and refer to the earlier unpublished manuscript when necessary.
45 "August2020," https://www.august2020.info/de/detail-page/109, accessed 06/23/2022.
46 Kureichik, 97.

With this monologue, Kureichik establishes a number of critical ideas: the protestors weren't seasoned, habitual agitators, they were met with irrational violence by the regime for their basic demands, and the protestors formed a community of care that supported one another in the midst of the horrifying and surprising response by the regime. Throughout the play, these strains are repeated in various ways by characters ranging in age from 17 to 64. Many of the "characters" display shock at being "dragged by force,"[47] "tased with a stun gun,"[48] "constantly accosted with humiliating comments,"[49] hearing men howling in the hallways, and being told by the policemen, "They'll rape you at the Okrestina Street Prison, and then they'll kill you."[50] Through the voices of these arrested and brutalized protestors, Kureichik emphasizes the physical and psychological trauma so many endured following the elections.

While the frequency with which the characters speak of violence might suggest the play maintains a single tone, it is actually quite dynamic in tone, rhythm, narrative style, and characterization. The third character to appear in the play is Maryia Kalesnikava, the beloved symbol of the pro-democracy protests with her characteristic short blond hair, bright red lipstick in a smile, and often seen forming a heart with her two hands, even in the courtroom. When Kalesnikava was taken to the Ukrainian border to be forced into exile in September 2020, she tore up her passport and refused to leave Belarus.[51] In September 2021, she was sentenced to 11 years in prison for "conspiracy to seize power by an Unconstitutional means," "creation and leading of an extremist organization," and other charges.[52] In the play, Kureichik selects text from Kalesnikava that captures her fearlessness and directness as well as an ironic tone mocking the regime and enduring hope. Like most of the pieces Kureichik selected and edited for the play, Kalesnikava's speech moves through several distinctive tonal shifts to create character complexity and a balance of epic magnitude and intimacy. While he didn't write any of the language of the play, he edited the pieces with masterful dramaturgical craftsmanship.

---

47 Ibid., 100.
48 Ibid., 111.
49 Andrei Kureichik, *Voices of the New Belarus*, trans. John Freedman, unpublished manuscript, 7.
50 Kureichik, *Two Plays*, 100.
51 "Belarus: Maryia Kalesnikava and Maksim Znak Sentenced to Jail over Historic Protests," Amnesty International, September 6, 2021, https://www.amnesty.org/en/latest/news/2021/09/belarusian-opposition-leaders-maryia-kalesnikava-and-maksim-znak-sentenced-to-10-and-11-years-respectively/.
52 Ibid.

Critically, the play contains her direct accusations of the threats of her named interrogators: N. N. Karpenkov, the head of GUBOPIK special police forces; G. Kazakevich, First Deputy Minister of the police; and A. Yu. Pavlyuchenko, head of the Operations and Analysis Center.[53] Thus, Kureichik documents and highlights the role of these specific officials in the illegal activities of the regime. Beyond documentation of these details, Kureichik undermines these authorities through Kalesnikava's portrayal of the authorities with her sense of their ridiculousness and ignorance. She describes the "smoky, dim, dark corridors" almost laughingly, with portraits of the "Old Man," staring down among various KGB artifacts. "You felt as if you had been transported into an old Soviet film." Her descriptions show how out of sync the regime seemed with the younger generations. After poking fun at her captors, Kalesnikava's monologue shifts to a call to determination, hope, and human dignity. "We are strong, brave and wise. We are together, and love is stronger than fear."[54]

While each piece is distinctive in tone, shape, size, and characterization, two more pieces help demonstrate the full dimension and scope of the play. Scene 11 of the play is one of the shortest monologues. It is based on a letter from a 28-year-old journalist and blogger, Ihar Losik, arrested in June 2020, after his 42-day hunger strike had ended. Losik began his hunger strike as new charges continued to be lodged against him while in Akrestsina prison. A mass letter-writing campaign was organized by pro-democracy forces to urge Losik to end his hunger strike. He eventually ended it, due to the "unbelievable wave of solidarity."[55] Nevertheless, the hunger strike seemed to take its toll on Losik, who remained despondent. In the play, he notes, "[…] when it seems it can't possibly get any worse, it gets even worse still."[56] His letter is the single scene in the play that depicts such hopelessness and despair.

The final scene in the play captures the feeling of love and pride and hopeful solidarity in a letter from Vitold Ashurak to his mother from prison. Ashurak, a coordinator of the For Freedom movement in Lida, was serving a five-year sentence. In his letter, he tells his mother that he has received so many letters of support from Belarusians all over the world. "Mom! People respect me! You raised me correctly!"[57] With certainty, Ashurak assures

---

53 Kureichik, 102.
54 Ibid.
55 "Jailed Belarusian Blogger Ends Hunger Strike after 42 Days," *Barron's*, January 25, 2021, https://www.barrons.com/news/jailed-belarusian-blogger-ends-hunger-strike-after-42-days-01611597905.
56 Kureichik, 123.
57 Ibid., 143.

his mother that he'll come home. "Change is coming. It will bring freedom to me, and it will bring me home to you!"[58] Ashurak died in prison on May 21, 2021, officially of a heart attack, but his body was reportedly returned to his family with his head completely bandaged.[59] Kureichik ends the play on this complex dualism of Ashurak's encouraging and assuring tone blended with the audience's understanding that he had been beaten to death. It's a powerful and heartrending testimonial, a dramatic call to action, and an act of mourning and remembrance.

As with *Insulted. Belarus.*, the play premiered on September 10, 2021, in Kherson, Ukraine, at the Mikola Kulish Academic Theatre, directed by Siarhei Pavliuk, at the 23rd International Melpomene Tavrii Theatre Festival.[60] Actors from the theatre, alongside Andrei and his son 14-year-old son Gleb, presented the work on an outdoor stage. Dressed in white and wearing white masks with red tape over their mouths, the actors stood in a tight group among white mannequins with strips of red tape over their mouths and hearts, and binding their hands together. On a screen at the back of the stage, images of the events in Belarus in 2020 ran throughout the production to capture the documentary nature of the play. Actors held photographs of the real-life person they portrayed. For the final, heartbreaking scene of Ashurak's text, Pavlyuk chose to have the mother appear dressed in black mourning clothes— in contrast to the other performers, reading her son's letter beside a headless, discolored mannequin with Ashurak's photograph taped to its chest. This stylized approach enabled the gap between representation and reality, important for a documentary piece of this nature, which, unlike most documentary films, is removed from the realm of the authentic through reenactment. The meta-theatrical gesture blended with verbatim text and documentary footage generates a Brechtian critical distance allowing audiences to absorb the stories without being overwhelmed by empathy into inaction.

Like *Insulted. Belarus.*, *Voices of the New Belarus* inspired a wide range of interpretive approaches and documentary performance styles. Following the opening in Ukraine, theatre groups and companies in Poland, Finland, Germany, Taiwan, the UK, and the United States presented live readings, digital versions, installations, and film adaptations of the play in 2021.

---

58 Ibid., 144.
59 "Body of Jailed Belarusian Activist Reportedly Returned with Bandaged Head," *Radio Free Europe/Radio Liberty*, May 25, 2021, https://www.rferl.org/a/belarus-political-prisoner-dead-bandaged-head/31273419.html.
60 "Premiere of Andrei Kureichik's New Documentary Play," Artists at Risk, https://artistsatrisk.org/2021/09/10/press-premiere-of-andrei-kureichiks-new-documentary-play-voices-of-new-belarus-in-ukraine/?lang=en.

Insulted. Belarus. Dir. Siarhei Pavliuk, Photos by Mikola Kulish Theatre (Kherson, Ukraine).

Directors often rearranged the individual scenes depending on the impact they wanted to achieve, many included documentary footage of the 2020 protests, and most found ways to signal the actors as performers representing real living and deceased persons. Many productions maintained Kureichik's narration and some included his comments in the script's foreword.

Once again, Oskana Mysina made a film of Kureichik's film, using similar strategies for filming individual scenes and rhythmic editing. The casting alone added interpretive layers. Exiled Belarusian artists were featured including actress and journalist, Anna Sirotina, who presented Maryia Kalesnikava, and Vladimir Shcherban, former director of the Belarus Free Theatre and founder of Hunch Theatre in London, gave a touching representation of Alexei Berezinsky who sent good wishes to his mother, family members, and all Belarusian women on International Women's Day through *Novy Chas* newspaper from his prison cell. The cast included renowned Russian director and actor Konstantin Raikin, who performed the role of Vitold Ashurak, placed as scene 2. Raikin, seated in front of a camera in a small, enclosed room, read Ashurak's hopeful letter to his mother, skillfully capturing the dissonance of the letter and the nightmarish fact of his brutal death. Using slight vocal gestures—sighs, throat clearing, choking back tears—Raikin never allows the audience to fall into the letter's optimistic outlook. Mysina also cast real political figures and journalists in the film, including Belarusian Olga Karach, now living in Poland, and Russian opposition politician Ilya Yashin, arrested and imprisoned in Russia himself in July 2022, following his public anti-war comments. The film had its theatrical screening premiere at the Reva and David Logan Center for the Arts, University of Chicago, on May 18, 2022. Kureichik gave a post-screening talkback, attended by artists, historians, scholars, and members of the group, Belarusians of Chicago. The film generated a lively discussion and audience members expressed deep gratitude to Kureichik for documenting these events, raising awareness, and remembering the political prisoners and Ashurak.[61]

With these two works, Kureichik and Freedman mobilized a powerful and far-reaching network of theatre artists. The bodies of actors from Nigeria, Hong Kong, the United States, and across Europe have stood in for those who are displaced, locked away, and made invisible or ungrievable by the Belarusian State. In presenting these real figures, they can continue to speak and be heard in ways that unsettle the regime's efforts to silence and remove these figures from the public square. Additionally, these works in production resonated more broadly than imagined, enabling communities to engage around political injustice and police brutality globally. They serve as models for activating community engagement, contesting State propaganda, and using performance as a protest through assembly. Kureichik currently lives in exile in the United States, where he was recently a Maurice Greenberg Yale World Scholar, and continues to use performance as a means of combatting authoritarianism and drawing attention to Belarusian political prisoners.

---

61 The author coordinated and attended this event.

Chapter 2

A TIME FOR THEATRE: *COURAGE* AND THE BELARUS FREE THEATRE

What we are seeing when bodies assemble on the street, in the square, or in other public venues is the exercise—one might call it performative— of the right to appear, a bodily demand for a more livable set of lives.[1]

Judith Butler, *Notes Toward a Performative Theory of Assembly*, 2015

But now [...] What good is theatre?

Pavel Haradnizky, *Courage*, 2021

Late in the documentary film *Courage* directed by Aliaksei Paluyan, actor Pavel Haradnizky, who has been cleaning his apartment and contemplating emigration, thinks about the role of theatre in the midst of the political protests that erupted in Belarus following the 2020 Presidential elections. He considers the state of Belarus, saying it is no longer just a dictatorship, but a "complete tyranny."

> Back when times were more "liberal," we could express truths between the lines. But now [...] what good is theatre? [...] There's no time for theatre in Belarus right now. When the situation changes, the need for theatre, contemplation and thoughts will rise again. That's why theatre won't disappear.[2]

Filmed amidst the turmoil surrounding the elections, the documentary captures the shifting emotional states and trauma of alienation through the eyes of three actors of the Belarus Free Theatre. Despite Haradnizky's skepticism about the usefulness of performance and art in such a crisis,

1 Judith Butler, *Notes Toward a Performative Theory of Assembly* (Cambridge, MA and London: Harvard University Press, 2015), 25.
2 *Courage*, dir. Aliaksei Paluyan, Living Pictures Productions, 2021.

Courage, Living Pictures Productions Gbr.

the film itself makes the case for the power and value of such work. Throughout the unnarrated film, built on a series of fragmented scenes of daily life and footage from scenes of mass protest, Paluyan also depicts segments from Belarus Free Theatre performances. Glimpses of these plays, themselves built on documentary events of the Belarusian past, reveal the ways in which these performances invited audiences to commune, remain engaged, remember, mourn, and heal. While the performances help mobilize communities, they also make lives grievable that the State otherwise designates as disposable. The film and the performances it features strip away romantic notions of revolution while portraying the ongoing struggle for human rights, dignity, and democracy in Belarus. This chapter analyzes both the film and the theatre performances it captures as part of documenting the resistance. Looking both at the documentary material depicted along with the aesthetic choices of presentation in their historical contexts, the chapter reinforces the particular value of theatre in a time of crisis.

Courage, which premiered at the Berlin International Film Festival in June 2021, centers on the experiences of three long-time actors of the underground Belarus Free Theatre during the anxious lead-up to the elections and the surprising show of solidarity in the face of the authoritarian's brutal response. Paluyan filmed Pavel Haradnizky, Dzianis Tarasenka, and Maryna Yakubovich in their homes, at work in and outside the theatre, at the protests, and in various modes of transportation traversing the city. Through the experiences of these artists, the film depicts the uneasy blend of activism and domestic life in the midst of the ongoing crisis. The choice to build the film around these performers, who emerge as both average citizens and leading figures, amplifies the significance of the arts in mobilizing resistance. As Sviatlana Tsikhanouskaya said prior to the film's premiere at the Berlin International Film Festival in June 2021, "Artists played a tremendous role in the protests," and noted the particular power of the arts in building solidarity.[3] While a focus on the three performers provides basic shape and a sense of narrative to the film, Paluyan doesn't attempt to tell the individual stories of these three; rather, they become touchstones for a film that unobtrusively captures the shifting scenes, sense of growing social solidarity, and the emotional turbulence of the nonviolent uprising against the oppressive State.

In one scene in the film after the 2020 protests had begun, cofounder of the Belarus Free Theatre Nicolai Khalezin speaks to the actors in Minsk virtually from London, where he has been working via Skype with the theatre since emigrating in 2010. He and cofounder Natalia Kaliada, his wife, encourage the actors to write a lot and record how they feel, make note of what has changed, and what is going on to capture the pivotal moment. "It's a paradigm shift," said Khalezin, who had spent time in prison for participating in earlier protests in Belarus. The theatre leaders wanted to document the moment-to-moment emotional shifts of those who were experiencing the events. When were they skeptical? When afraid? When hopeful and resolved? When frightened and considering emigration? With his film *Courage*, Paluyan captures what Khalezin had asked the actors to record with pen and paper.

Aliaksei Paluyan, a screenwriter and director previously known for his 2017 short films *Lake of Happiness* and *Krajžančyn: Country of Women*, began filming members of the Belarus Free Theatre in rehearsal and performance two years before the August 2020 elections. Paluyan had followed the work of the theatre after attending a performance many years earlier. For the film, Paluyan first worked with German Director of Photography Jesse Mazuch, who helped capture Minsk's Soviet-style cityscapes, external order, and preelection rhythms of life. For safety, Mazuch left Belarus when the momentum of the protests grew, but Paluyan remained determined to film the events in spite of the danger. Belarusian Tanya Haurylchyk took over as Director of Photography, capturing the frenetic shift and uncertainties amidst the protests. As Colette De Castro noted in the *East European Film Bulletin*, "the change in camerawork mirrors the situation in Belarus, where resistance stayed hidden from sight until it finally exploded into

---

3 Torsten Landsberg and Scott Roxborough, "'Courage' on the Front Lines of the Belarus Protests," *DW*, June 11, 2021, https://www.dw.com/en/courage-on-the-frontline-of-the-belarus-protests/a-57843164.

the streets."[4] Paluyan had anticipated a growing resistance movement during the elections and in the face of ongoing conversations around integration with Russia, but he was surprised by how quickly the protests grew.[5] Paluyan and Haurylchyk knew they could be arrested and detained, along with other journalists and filmmakers on the scene, but managed to navigate the environment throughout August. Paluyan emigrated to Germany in September 2020, keeping the film footage safe, and began the process of editing and finalizing the film.

Courage opens with footage from late 1990s protests against Lukashenka's regime and the high-profile disappearances of political dissidents interspersed with clips of police beating protestors with batons. The film then shifts to quiet shots of orderly traffic and contemporary Minsk cityscapes in the shadow of the Soviet Union. Soviet-era murals and monuments mark the landscape, where buildings still proclaim, "Glory to the Victors," in reference to World War II. The whole sequence magnifies a description of Minsk written by Masha Gessen in 2020.

> If you are a visitor to Minsk, the capital of Belarus, you see wide clean avenues and a moderate quantity of signs of life: a little traffic, a minimum street activity, a smattering of restaurants. It's like it hasn't been over a quarter of a century since the Soviet Union collapsed— more like it ducked out for a smoke and is coming right back.[6]

Opening the film with scenes of these settled, orderly, lethargic spaces allows Paluyan to show how the space transforms as a new public materializes, demanding acknowledgment and the right to be seen and heard. He captures what Butler calls the reconfiguring and refunctioning of the material environment through the actions of protestors.[7]

Following these establishing shots, the film introduces actor Pavel Haradnizky in his apartment, playing a folk song on the piano and hanging

---

4 Colette De Castro, "Subterranean Explosion: Aliaksei Paluyan's *Courage*," *East European Film Bulletin* Vol. 116 (Summer 2021), https://eefb.org/perspectives/aliaksei-paluyans-courage-2021/.

5 Ola Salwa, "Aliaksei Paluyan and Jörn Möllenkamp, director and producer of Courage," *Cineuropa*, March 17, 2021, https://cineuropa.org/en/interview/398912/.

6 Gessen, Masha, "What you see is nothing," Introduction to Misha Friedman, Two Women in Their Time: The Belarus Free Theatre and the Art of Resistance," The New Press, 2020: 8.

7 Judith Butler, *Notes Toward a Performative Theory of Assembly* (Cambridge, MA and London: Harvard UP, 2015), 72.

his wet clothes to dry on the lines strung up above the bathroom tub. Maryna Yakubovich and Dzianis Tarasanka are introduced in similarly undramatic environments: Maryna feeds and chats with her toddler and Dzianis sands a car in the autobody shop where he has worked since leaving the theatre three years earlier. Without guiding narration, the film moves from depicting daily life and rehearsals or performances to scenes of the growing protests and increasing police presence as the three performers express uncertainty about the future. Two pivotal scenes anchor the film, capturing the energy and uncertainty of the moment, the blend of fear, hope, and courage. The first is when a group of protestors urge young soldiers to join them, placing flowers in their shields. For just a moment, it seems the two groups could align. But this hopeful moment is shattered by the arrival of more security forces and their harsh presentation. The second critical scene occurs when loved ones visit a detention center in search of their missing children, friends, and partners. When the prisoners are released, there are bursts of applause, joy, recognition, and honor, surprising those who were detained and endured the unimaginable. The film ends with footage from a performance of a 12-year-old documentary play by the Belarus Free Theatre which echoed the current moment, showing Belarusian dissidents' desperate search for answers and hope on stage and in the audience. At the time of Paluyan's departure from Belarus in September 2020, much hope remained, but the number of protestors had begun to dwindle as the government became increasingly ruthless with arrests and eventually closed all civic organizations supportive of the protestors. By December 2020, due to the imprisonment or emigration of key leaders, ongoing suppression by the security forces, and support of Vladimir Putin, the movement was effectively suppressed.[8]

In the film, Paluyan demonstrates how Belarusians anticipated unrest before the elections through the unease of all three actors in the lead-up to the elections. The actors are largely guarded about the likelihood of fair elections and skeptical that anything will change significantly. In one conversation, after Dzianis has voted, Pavel prompts, "What if they do it fairly?" referring to the election commission, and Dzianis replies, "I don't trust them."[9] He believes the numbers have been predetermined, as Kureichik portrayed in *Insulted. Belarus*. Nevertheless, Dzianis lightly plucks out the song, "Mury," the 1970s Polish protest song adopted by the 2020 Belarusian pro-democracy resistance, on his guitar. Pavel joins him on his piano.

---

8 David R. Marples, "Changing Belarus," *Canadian Slavonic Papers* 63, nos. 3–4 (2021): 278–295.

9 *Courage*, dir. Aliaksei Paluyan, Living Pictures Productions, 2021.

Courage, Living Pictures Productions Gbr.

This hesitant sign of hope for change later morphs into outright belief. As the resistance gains momentum, all three actors betray unchecked optimism and sheer joy as they join the vast crowds joining the protests. Like others, they were surprised and emboldened by the large number of protestors showing up throughout Belarus. Maryna, smiling as she carries her flag through the city, challenges her earlier doubt about how the protest movement could possibly work. Pavel, on the phone with Dzianis, encourages him to come to the protests with "We are making history."

Several times in the film, Nicolai Khalezin, who suspects the actor-protestors could be in danger, appears on Skype to prepare the theatre workers in case they are arrested or need to flee the country. He reveals that preparations have been made to provide legal and financial support, as well as assistance to leave, if necessary. Khalezin warns that some members must not join the protests for fear that the entire company could be arrested. Even as the surprise and joy at the size of the movement reach the artistic directors in London, and they, too, understand the magnitude of the shift in the consciousness of Belarusians, they continue careful monitoring of the ensemble members and try to ensure their safety.

A number of key themes emerge through the loosely curated film including ideas of change, generational responsibility, communities of support, and the role of art in a dictatorship. Central to the film is the concept of change. It seems, at its heart, to pose the question, "Can anything change in Belarus?" while demonstrating that in some ways it has already, though the regime's response to opposition remains the same. Opening the film with earlier footage of police brutality against protesters, a clip of Lukashenka in younger days, and protestors creating a human chain indicates the cyclical nature of these events. It demonstrates the legacy of the protest movement as well as the predictable response of the regime. Later in the film, Dzianis listens as a 2020 protester describes his prison internment, and he notes, "Nothing has changed since 1994." Generations of officers pass down the exact same techniques, he explains. "There's no creativity whatsoever.[...] It's boring."[10] Yet, he adds, that 2010 was brutal but 2020 is much worse. As we have seen, Khalezin, arrested and beaten in 2010, called 2020 "a paradigm shift."[11] He remained optimistic that change is possible in Belarus, in spite of the cycle of protests and violent suppression of dissent and the cynicism it has fostered.

When it becomes clear the government has overpowered the resistance, Maryna and her husband debate whether to stay and try to change the country or emigrate for the future of their child. They feel they must decide between staying to fight for a potential new future for their county, where generations before them had failed, or the immediate future and safety of their child. The film depicts their vulnerability and precarity as they face unpredictability regardless of which path they choose. Throughout the film, though, Paluyan depicts Maryna and the other artists engaged in actions— underground performances or participating in protests—that demonstrate a defiance of this vulnerability, leveraging it, through assembly.

The Belarus Free Theatre

The Belarus Free Theatre, cofounded by Natalia Kaliada and Nicolai Khalezin, officially launched in March 2005 in Minsk in support of playwrights and artists who had begun to defy strict censorship in Belarus. A journalist, editor, and long-time political activist, Khalezin turned to the theatre after his independent news organizations kept being shut down by the authorities; an underground theatre could be more nimble than a press. Along with diplomat Kaliada, who became a producer and writer, they began to cultivate a company of artists. Hosting the First International Contest of Contemporary Drama, an online forum featuring artists from 12 post-Soviet countries, on March 30, 2005, marked the group's first major event, championed by Vaclav Havel and Tom Stoppard.[12] By May 2005, director Vladimir Shcherban joined Kaliada and Khalezin, and together the company began to develop a stylized aesthetic and physical theatrical

---

10 *Courage*, dir. Aliaksei Paluyan, Living Pictures Productions, 2021.

11 Ibid.

12 Khalezin, Nicolai, *Belarus Free Theatre Staging a Revolution: New Plays from Eastern Europe* (London: Oberon Books, 2016), vi.

vocabulary that captured what Noah Birksted-Breen has called "the collective psychosis" of individuals trapped in oppressive regimes.[13] Working in various underground spaces, including apartments, clubs, and garages transformed into theatrical spaces, the group performed taboo plays like Sarah Kane's *4:48 Psychosis* and devised works from oral histories and autobiographical materials, such as Khalezin's *Generation Jeans* and Kaliada's *They Saw Dreams*. Productions of the company are characterized by intensely physical, expressionist performance elements (sharp and contrasting gestures, lighting and sound; ritualistic movement and song; and nightmarish and provocative symbolism) blended with documentary-style realism and the use of digital montage and projections.

Following the December 2010 elections in Belarus, Khalezin and Kaliada, who had both been arrested and released for participating in protests, left Belarus with Shcherban and members of the company for the Under the Radar Festival in New York City.[14] The troupe, which included Haradnitsky, Tarasenka, and Yakubovich (then Yurevich), performed *Being Harold Pinter* and *Zone of Silence*, both directed by Shcherban, at the festival to great acclaim in January 2011.[15] Following the tour, at a London layover on their return trip home, they were warned not to return to Belarus due to threats of imprisonment.[16] The Khalezin, Kaliada, and Shcherban emigrated to London, where they continued to develop productions via Skype with members of the company who remained underground in Minsk.

Throughout *Courage*, scenes of rehearsal and performance of works by the Belarus Free Theatre are interwoven into the film's loose narrative. *Zone of Silence, Time of Women, Dogs of Europe,* and *Discover Love* built on interviews and documentary materials feature prominently. Incorporating these performance clips into the film created a palimpsest highlighting the recurring cycles of stasis, protest, and crackdowns in Belarus since the 1990s as well as the ongoing

---

Noah Birksted-Breen, "Living in the Skin of Dictatorship: An Encounter with Belarus Free Theatre," *Cultural Geographies in Practice* (2022): 485–492, 487.

Larry Rohter, "Theatre Group in Belarus Is Forced Underground," *New York Times*, December 21, 2010, https://www.nytimes.com/2010/12/22/theater/22radar.html.

David Sheward, "Being Harold Pinter," *Backstage*, Updated August 15, 2012, https://www.backstage.com/magazine/article/harold-pinter-59457/; Ben Brantley, "Political Theatre, Brought to You by the Politically Powerless," *New York Times*, January 6, 2011, https://www.nytimes.com/2011/01/07/theater/reviews/07pinter.html.

The film, *Connection*, dir. Vladimir Shcherban, featuring Khalezin and Jude Law, depicts the London layover and decision to emigrate. "Connection: a short film starring Jude Law." Dir. Vladimir Shcherban, *The Guardian*, September 16, 2013, https://www.theguardian.com/stage/video/2013/sep/16/connection-jude-law-video.

A TIME FOR THEATRE

cultural resistance. The reiterative nature of the protests in Lukashenka's Belarus might evoke despair, but the very act of reproducing them demonstrates the longevity of the movement and the enduring refusal to relent. As Butler points out, the bodies assembled in protest say, "We are still here, persisting, demanding greater justice, a release from precarity, a possibility of a livable life."[17] Pointing to the recurrence of such action in the film and in the plays of the Belarus Free Theatre reveals such persistence.

The Belarus Free Theatre's *Time of Women*

Time of Women, set in 2014, depicts the intersections between the present lives of three women who are haunted by their imprisonment in Belarus in 2010 for protesting the presidential elections. Based on interviews with the women and other historical documents, the play focuses on the journalists Iryna Khalip and Natalya Radina and political activist Nasta Palazhanka. The play premiered in a small apartment, a secret location, in Minsk in 2014. Since then, a filmed version of that production has circulated online as part of various festivals and revivals meant to stir renewed interest in Belarus's political prisoners and human rights violations under Lukashenka. The play was performed live at the Young Vic in London in 2015 and at New York's Under the Radar Festival in 2017. On both occasions, the productions received a notable critical reception that helped raise the international profile (and considerable leverage) of the ensemble.

The play captures decisive moments in the lives and friendship of three prominent political dissidents, who were all forced into exile after their imprisonment. The journalist Iryna Khalip is perhaps the best known internationally. At the time of her arrest in 2010, Iryna Khalip was the Belarus correspondent for the Moscow-based independent newspaper *Novaya Gazeta*. In 2009, the International Women's Media Foundation awarded her the "Courage in Journalism" award for her work with the paper, although she received anonymous death threats for her investigative work on Belarusian governmental corruption. Khalip's husband, Andrei Sannikov, the primary opposition candidate for President of Belarus in 2010 and founder of the pro-democracy news organization Charter 97, was imprisoned for organizing and participating in a mass riot. He served 16 months in prison before his release. Khalip, who along with her husband was beaten and arrested at a December protest in 2010, spent two weeks in prison and served several months in house arrest under a two-year suspended sentence. While she and her husband were

---

17 Butler, *Notes*, 25.

in prison, the authorities threatened to place her three-year-old son, who lived with her mother, in a state facility. The play highlights these events through scenes of her interrogation. In 2013, Khalip received the PEN Pinter Prize, along with long-time supporter Tom Stoppard, for her commitment to freedom of expression.[18]

Natalya Radzina, editor-in-chief of Sannikov's independent news website Charter 97, was arrested in her office along with her colleagues in December 2010, following the protests against the regime for the fraudulent elections. After a month in prison, she was released on house arrest. She fled Belarus in 2011. Poland and later Lithuania granted her asylum, yet she continued to receive death threats for her work exposing corruption and human rights' violations in Belarus, which she continued through Charter 97. In 2011, she received an International Press Freedom award from the Committee to Protect Journalists.[19]

Nasta Palazhanka is best known for her work with the opposition youth movement, the Young Front, which she joined at age 14, to help promote democratic values and civil society. She had been arrested and imprisoned several times before her detention in 2010. Notably, she became engaged to the Young Front's leader Zmitser Dashkevich and married him while he served a prison sentence in Hrodna. Nasta was awarded a Woman of Courage Award in 2011, at a reception hosted by Hillary Clinton, although the imprisoned Palazhanka was unable to attend.[20] She and Zmitser continued their civic activities and were both convicted again in 2022 for "participation in actions that grossly violate public order," for which he received an 18-month prison sentence and she was sentenced to three years of house arrest.[21]

The original production, written by Khalezin and Kaliada, and directed by Khalezin through Skype rehearsals in 2014, interwove the stories of the three 2010 political prisoners. In the initial underground production in a Minsk apartment, the small performance space was divided into three sections: a central "present" living room area with a rug and small table

18 Liz Bury, "Irina Khalip Wins PEN Pinter Prize for International Writer of Courage," *The Guardian*, October 9, 2013, https://www.theguardian.com/books/2013/oct/09/irina-khalip-pen-pinter-prize-tom-stoppard.

19 Committee to Protect Journalists, "Natalya Radina, Belarus, 2011 CPJ International Press Freedom Awardee," https://cpj.org/awards/natalya-radina-belarus/.

20 "Secretary Clinton to Host 2011 International Women of Courage Awards with Special Guest First Lady Michelle Obama on March 8," U.S. Department of State website, March 4, 2011, https://2009-2017.state.gov/r/pa/prs/ps/2011/03/157710.htm.

21 "Zmitser Dashkevich," Viasna Human Rights Center, https://prisoners.spring96.org/en/person/zmicer-daszkevicz.

stand with a miniature Christmas tree; an interrogation office with a desk, bright lamp, and two chairs on the left; and to the right, a light, metal-framed bunk bed representing the Amerikanka prison room. The setting bumped up against the small audience space, where American critic Ben Brantley recalled about 30 audience members, who had to be carefully and secretly guided into the apartment, sat "thigh-to-thigh" on make-shift benches and the floor.[22] The action of the play moves fluidly between the prison and living room punctuated sharply by the three individual interrogations of the women during their time in prison. These interrogations haunt the women, who were threatened with violence, sexual violence, and harm to their families for their participation in the protests.

The cast included Maryia Sazonava as Iryna, Maryna (Yurevich) Yakubovich as Natalya, and Yana Rusakevich (also featured in *Courage*) as Nasta. Actor Kiryl Kanstantsi played the KGB interrogator, Colonel Orlov. The early performance style of the Belarus Free Theatre blended everyday realism with heightened physical action. In *Time of Women*, stylized action and psychological gesture allow the performance to expand beyond the confines of the small acting space. Two examples illustrate the way the performers extend verbatim texts through physical gestures as a shorthand for complex psychology. As he begins the first interrogation, Kiryl Kanstantsi portrays Orlov with increasingly rapid speech as he encircles the desk and then suddenly bursts into three deep squats with his arms thrusting forward as if warming up for a sporting event. The physical action very quickly reveals the inner psychology of the character, who sees this terrifying work as a kind of sport and creates a sense of impending horror that traumatizes his victims. Another example of this performance approach occurs when the actress Maryna Yakubovich utters a four-minute monologue about her experiences while hula-hooping a large metal hoop. As it encircles her, the hoop mirrors her experience of feeling trapped in an inescapable loop. These kinds of effects highlight the documentary event as a performance and capture aspects of the unspoken, psychological and physiological realities of the characters.

The Belarus Free Theatre's *Discover Love*

Courage also features scenes from BFT's play, *Discover Love*, originally written and directed by Nikolai Khalezin in 2008. The play centers on

---

22 Ben Brantley, "Theatre Banned in Belarus but the Show Goes On," *New York Times*, October 14, 2015, https://www.nytimes.com/2015/10/18/theater/banned-in-belarus-but-the-shows-go-on.html.

Irina Krasovskaya, the wife of Belarusian businessman and pro-democracy advocate, Anatoly Krasovsky, who was kidnapped and presumably murdered, along with politician Viktar Hanchar, by the Belarusian security forces on September 16, 1999.[23] The disappearances of Krasovsky and Hanchar and the State's failure to investigate have been a fundamental issue around which pro-democracy activists in Belarus have mobilized. Irina Krasovskaya, who founded the We Remember Foundation in Washington, DC after she emigrated, attended the world premiere of the play and has supported the company's human rights efforts. The play is often presented in association with the Global Artistic Campaign in support of the UN Convention against Enforced Disappearances.[24]

The production, which has continued to evolve, begins and ends with selected statements from the "UN Declaration on the Protection of All Persons from Enforced Disappearance."[25] The play opens with an indistinct male voiceover stating,

> "enforced disappearance" is considered to be the arrest, detention, abduction or any other form of deprivation of liberty by agents of the State or by persons or groups of persons acting with the authorization, support or acquiescence of the State, followed by a refusal to acknowledge the deprivation of liberty or by concealment of the fate or whereabouts of the disappeared person, which place such a person outside the protection of the law.

The text comes from Part I, Article II of the declaration. While the play centers on Irina and Anatoly, the production expands to include a section on Father Jerzy Popiełuszko, the Polish Roman Catholic Priest whose popular sermons in the early 1980s focused on human rights and peaceful resistance. He disappeared and was murdered in 1984. The production of *Discover Love* also recognizes thousands of other disappeared persons through film footage and a recitation of numbers of those disappeared across the globe.

---

23 "Former Belarusian Police Officer Says He Was Involved in the Killing of Lukashenko Critics," *Voice of America*, December 17, 2019, https://www.voanews.com/a/europe_ former-belarusian-police-officer-says-he-was-involved-killing-lukashenko-critics/ 6181203.html.

24 https://belarusfreetheatre.com/campaigns/global-artists-for-solidarity-with-belarus.

25 My discussion of the production is based on the recording of the production on Vimeo, https://vimeo.com/belarusfreetheatre/review/153098041/bdf4a104ba, accessed 02/12/2023.

Built on fragmented scenes from her life in Belarus and narrated by Irina, played by Maryna Yakubovich, the play focuses on State-enforced disappearances of dissidents and the loved ones left searching for answers. The ensemble includes Yakubovich, Pavel Haradnitski, and Aleh Sidorchyk who play multiple characters throughout the 80-minute show. The sparse stage includes a basic mattress on a wooden frame to the right and a simple dining chair at the center of the stage. The actors change the bedding on the mattress to signify time and setting shifts—from Irina's childhood home with her grandmother in Volozhin, Belarus, to the upscale apartment in Minsk that she and Anatoly finally secure after years of financial struggle.

The first third of the play highlights Irina's childhood in Belarus. As Irina recounts her joyful childhood in several scenes, she highlights memories of food—especially the rare pleasure of oranges, trips to the circus, bedtime stories in Belarusian on the radio, and her first elementary school crush. Through Irina's grandmother, the history of terror in the region is established as an undercurrent. Grandmother lived through the revolution and she lost her husband and daughter during World War II, though she survived the Nazi occupation and then the Communist party repression. She fictionalized her past to protect her children. Though these tragic details slip through, the scene between Irina and her grandmother is loving, playful, and light.

The next section of the play focuses on Irina's relationship with Anatoly (Tolya). "Everything in my life began only when I met Tolya," she tells the audience.[26] In an extended introduction to their relationship (which turns out to be Irina's dream), the actors portraying Tolya and Irina (Sidorchyk and Yurevich) dance a sensual tango and kiss passionately, demonstrating the intensity of her desire for him, her physics teacher. They meet again later and eventually marry in a decidedly unromantic ceremony and struggle through many years of low-income domestic stress before Anatoly finally achieves success in business. Irina narrates the final years of their life together as filled with freedom and love.

The final section of the play shifts sharply, marked by Tolya's line, "And then I was killed."[27] In transition, a distorted video of a carousel plays as Sidorchyk repeatedly throws himself down on the darkened stage, struggles to get up, and falls again as if by force. He then upends the mattress and moves the large metal wheels holding it to form a cross upstage. He places

---

26 Ibid.
27 Ibid.

a small basin of water upstage. The actor Haradnitski arrives as a Belarusian security officer in a black balaclava and clothing and forces Tolya in front of him, facing the audience on his knees. As Tolya narrates his kidnapping and torture, the officer stands behind him squeezing orange juice from oranges on the screaming Tolya. This symbolic portrayal of violence, characteristic of the Belarus Free Theatre, captures the terror but creates aesthetic distance for the audience to process.

After what is ultimately seen as an execution that parallels a crucifixion, the scene shifts to the narrative of Father Popiełuszko. The actors then recite a prayer that includes phrases, "Mother of all who've been interrogated, pray for us; Mother of all who speak the truth, pray for us; Mother of all who resist, pray for us [...]." Projections of Father Popiełuszko and others who have disappeared appear at the end of the prayer, while a voice-over loop from the UN Declaration on enforced disappearance plays. The performance ends when Yakubovich, as Irina, introduces herself and talks about the work she does to keep the memory of Anatoly alive. As a performance of documentary theatre, the piece effectively continues the mission of the company and Irina Krasorskaya to raise awareness, hold lost loved ones in memory, and mourn together.

The Belarus Free Theatre's *Dogs of Europe*

Courage also features the Belarus Free Theatre production of *Dogs of Europe*. Although the play is not a documentary theatre piece, it does use footage from the massive August 2020 protests and resonates deeply with life under the authoritarian regime in Belarus, where civil society was completely crushed and dissidents were effectively silenced by the end of that year. The play is an adaptation of the 2017 dystopian novel by Belarusian Alhierd Baharevic, a highly lauded author who was forced to flee Belarus, where his novel was banned, following the 2020 elections. The futuristic novel takes place from 2019 to 2049, during the formation of the fictional New Reich of the Russian State, where there is no free press or right to assemble and the judicial system, along with the military and educational institutions, are tightly controlled by the State. Pre-show projections explain, "Any manifestation of free thinking is punishable by imprisonment or the death penalty."[28] As Arifa Akbar points out in her review of the production at the Barbican in London in 2022, "every member of the ensemble has spent time in jail [...]" thus the fictional and

---

28 "Dogs of Europe," video recording of the Belarus Free Theatre production at the Barbican Theatre in London, March 2022, https://vimeo.com/703733978.

real worlds overlap through the production, which ended with a short, direct appeal to the audience by co-director Natalia Kaliada.[29]

Kaliada and Khalezin adapted and directed the play, first performed underground in Minsk. In London, the production increased in scope and scale, expanding into a three-hour adaptation of the 900-page novel, with a large projection screen featuring imaginative moving collages and video footage underscoring the tonal shifts and intensifying horror of the world. The production opens with a mythical scene suggesting the birth and growth of fascism in Belarus. Next appears documentary footage from the 2020 protests and the Russian invasion of Ukraine in 2022, transitioning the play from the present into the future. The future presents a threatening New Reich, an expansive "Russian State" dominated by the Russian language and an oppressive, prohibitive culture, bordering a "League of European Nations" upon the collapse of the European Union.

The production advances through short symbolic or agitprop scenes alternating with haunting folk songs and rebellious hip-hop songs demonstrating the State's efforts to "eradicate the enemy" and "prevent social disorder."[30] As characters attempt to resist or become complicit in the new regime, the play grows increasingly violent, vigorously portrayed through heightened symbolic physical action. Strikingly, throughout the intermission, a nude actor runs continuously in a large circle on stage, sometimes crying out, but refusing to give up, refusing to disappear. The production, and Kaliada's curtain speech, urges immediate action and resistance to the current brutal Russian regime, supported by the Belarusian government, which threatens human rights and civil liberties and the future of Europe. In the film *Courage*, Paluyan crystallizes this warning in a portrayal of the three actors holding burning books.

After its premiere at the Berlin International Film Festival in March 2021, *Courage* continued to gain an international audience across Europe and in the United States. In order to protect those in the documentary who may have remained in Belarus, the film has not been widely distributed on streaming platforms. From July through August 2022, Paluyan toured for screenings in Dresden, Kassel, Tbilisi, Munich, Prague, and Warsaw. Paluyan was surprised and thrilled that Warsaw's 329-seat Kino Luna completely

29 Arifa Akbar, "Dogs of Europe review—Art and Activism Combine in Breathtaking Spectacle," *The Guardian*, March 13, 2022, https://www.theguardian.com/stage/2022/mar/13/dogs-of-europe-review-barbican-london-free-belarus-theatre.

30 "Dogs of Europe," video recording of the Belarus Free Theatre production at the Barbican Theatre in London, March 2022, https://vimeo.com/703733978.

sold out.[31] The screenings were accompanied by an action in which audience members raised the photographs of Belarusian political prisoners found in their seats. This collective action willfully resisted the public disappearance of Belarusian activists, rendering those lives visible and remembered. *Courage* was also screened in London, Stockholm, Sydney, Australia, and twice in Kiev in December 2022. Paluyan called these Ukrainian screenings among the most important screenings.[32] At the time the film was made, the world didn't yet understand the global implications of the 2020 Belarusian election and Lukashenka's support for Putin's war in Ukraine. The film won the Cinema for Peace Award for Political Film of the Year in 2022. Screenings continued in 2023, including in Paris and at Berlin's famous Maxim Gorki Theatre. Paluyan, who recently cofounded the Belarusian Film Academy, with Volia Chajkouskaya and Darya Zhuk, continues to fight censorship, promote screenings of the film, and stage collective action to ensure that audiences remember and know that many Belarusians oppose the current government in Belarus, complicit in the Russian war in Ukraine.[33]

"Courage," Paluyan said in a short documentary about himself in 2022, "is when you are afraid and sometimes lose hope but you keep doing it because it's not possible not to keep doing it."[34]

Acknowledging the persistence of Belarusian activists, his film historicizes and memorializes, makes room for mourning and remembering those whom the State would deny basic human recognition, and revives and extends the bond of social solidarity each time it is screened. The film also emphasizes the role of the theatre in creating and sustaining an active public, engaged together in acts of risk-taking through bodily presence and empathy, fortifying their resolve and right to remember.

---

31 Email to the author 08/12/2022.
32 Paluyan's FaceBook post on December 01, 2022.
33 Christopher Vourlias, "Filmmakers Launch Belarusian Film Academy to Give a Voice to Threatened Artists in Repressive Putin Ally," *Variety*, February 17, 2023, https://variety.com/2023/film/global/efm-belarusian-film-academy-1235526394/?fbclid=IwAR09O5iX13D9MAjNXsv3H5wfoIGDyR3xkpWOCXS2cKtApVjVT4B7aiBuBmE.
34 "Berlinale Talents 2022: Aliaksei Paluyan," short documentary, https://vimeo.com/676941002?fbclid=IwAR39kQMEauv4XnU716zOOCRxq-JHLArFCmBWdwjH5djgJVhxFllcYTBVVog.

AN INTERLUDE: INTERVIEW WITH VLADIMIR SHCHERBAN, COFOUNDER HUNCH THEATRE

VR: You emigrated to London on tour with the Belarus Free Theatre following the protests and violent aftermath of the 2010 Belarusian Presidential elections. You had previously worked as a director at the Yanka Kupala National Theatre. How would you describe the state of the theatre and censorship in Belarus prior to 2010?

VS: At the time of 2010, there were no truly independent theatre groups in Belarus; all theatres were state-owned and subordinate to the authorities. Therefore, the Belarusian theatre continued to exist in the Soviet format, where the stages were dominated by productions based on classical works or on plays by Soviet playwrights. Any allusions to the Belarusian reality were removed from the texts. Accordingly, the repertoires of the theatres practically lacked productions based on Belarusian contemporary playwrights. The main taboo was the real Belarusian with his real problems and daily challenges. It was with the emergence of new Belarusian playwrights, who began to reflect on the challenges of Belarusian reality in their works, that changes in the theatre landscape began and the image of a modern Belarusian appeared. Working at the National Theatre, I started doing readings and staging of their plays, which caused great interest on the part of the progressive public and, consequently, discontent and repression on the part of the management and authorities. As a result, I was dismissed from the state theatre, deprived of housing, and my name was removed from the posters of theatres. In fact, it was a ban on my profession; I could no longer work in state theatres and was forced to go completely underground, making and performing plays in private flats or clubs, under the guise of parties. But despite the risks and persecution by the authorities, it was in the underground that I found complete artistic freedom. Thus began my active collaboration with independent Belarusian playwrights and colleagues from the Free Theatre.

VR: You achieved international recognition as a cofounder and director of many of the BFT's celebrated productions, such as *Being Harold Pinter,*

King Lear, and *Zone of Silence*, among others. Many of your productions blend the autobiographical and biographical, the fictional, and the statistical in visually striking, physically demanding performances that represent the violence and cruelty of authoritarian states. In what way do you think the representation of the company's personal experiences in Belarus has been significant for its aesthetic?

VS: It was a fascinating and important artistic journey. Through contemporary British and then Belarusian dramaturgy, as a director together with the actors, I came to documentary and autobiographical, confessional theatre, came to ourselves. It was revolutionary for Belarusian theatre and for many Belarusians it changed forever the understanding of what theatre can be in principle. It was important for me to speak about myself in my performances, to speak with my own voice about the reality that surrounds us. Who are we, why is this happening to us, and where do we go from here? Together with the actors, we began to actively work with personal experience, in search of answers to these questions. In this way, the dividing line between actor and character, audience and action was erased. The spectators saw themselves in what was happening, and for many of them the performances themselves became oases of freedom, so many came to the performances repeatedly and found new facets in them. But it was not enough just to talk about ourselves, it became important to learn to work with the theme of violence that surrounds us from early childhood, whether it is domestic violence (*Zone of Silence*) or political, state violence (*Being Harold Printer*). It was important to talk about these themes, but also to find unique staging solutions, with the help of which the performers and the audience could overcome violence and achieve artistic catharsis. One of the most powerful expressive means is the search for a physical reaction, literally letting the theme pass through one's body and finding the reaction first of the body and then the birth of sound and words. All of these components struck expressive meanings that were born before the eyes of the viewer. The culmination of working with personal experience, physical theatre, and classical drama was *King Lear*, which I did at the Globe Theatre in London as part of the 2012 Theatre Olympiad.

VR: Do you think that the depiction of historical resistance in Belarus is significant for mourning and grieving loss while also building communities of care and support and ongoing resistance?

VS: Actors and directors are first and foremost citizens of their country, so it is our artistic and civic duty to remember those who have fallen in the struggle and to immortalize through various artistic means inspiring examples of resistance to violence. This opens up another important facet of art—therapeutic for both performers and audiences.

Vladimir Shcherban, Hunch Theatre Archive.

VR: Is there still the possibility for underground performances in Belarus, or has the regime essentially demolished the potential for any visible public resistance following the 2020 elections? Does virtual performance create an opening for community building?

VS: After 2020, the level of repression in Belarus has reached an unprecedented scale, comparable to Stalin's times, special services can easily stop you on the street and check your devices and applications you use. People are being thrown in jail for a comment or a like on social media. All independent media are recognized as "extremist." Thousands and thousands of creative people had to flee the country from the repression of the authorities. That's why today everyone in Belarus exists in survival mode and organizing underground performances is too risky for participants and spectators. Nevertheless, readings take place and with the help of new technologies, a new format of artistic interaction between creative people is constantly being sought. Even being in prison- actors, artists continue to create new works. This sad, but unique experience of Belarusian creators shows the whole world an example and returns to art its original creative and freedom-loving meaning.

VR: You appeared in Oksana Mysina's film of Andrei Kureichik's *Voices of the New Belarus*, a documentary piece recognizing the political prisoners in Belarus. Since the time of the filming, one participant, Russian politician Ilya Yashin, has been imprisoned and another, Liya Akhedzhakova, has been fired from her position at Moscow's Sovremennik Theatre for their anti-war statements. Did you imagine at the time that the aftermath of the 2020 Belarusian elections would give rise to Putin's path to war in Ukraine?

VS: Last summer, on the eve of the sad anniversary of the protests against the violence of the authorities in Belarus, I unexpectedly received a message proposal from Oksana Mysina. We didn't know each other personally at that time, but I immediately agreed. Because I knew Oksana as a unique actress and a caring person with an impeccable reputation.

Then I read Andrei Kureichik's script, which consists entirely of real letters/monologues of Belarusian political prisoners. Many of them are still in prison, some of them are no longer alive.... The monologues/ voices are sometimes confused, ragged, but piercing, like reality itself. And in this, I see a worthy continuation of the tradition of the outstanding Belarusian, Nobel laureate Sviatlana Aleksievich. Oksana and her husband John Freedman attracted incredible participants from different spheres to the project. Of course, while working on the film, we could not have imagined that there would be a war in Ukraine. It is all the more important to remember those who are now in prison in Belarus and whose voices are full of bitterness and hope.

VR: You recently cofounded HUNCHtheatre in London for live and virtual performances. Can you describe your hope for this new company?

VS: In 2018, I left the BFT and together with the British playwright and actor Oliver Bennett I formed an independent Hunch Theatre in London. A few months later, with our Belarusian colleagues, we opened a branch of the Hunch Theatre in Belarus and are working on creating a branch in Berlin. Therefore, each performance becomes a unique example of cultural and artistic exchange between creators from different countries with different political and social backgrounds. In the five years of the company's existence, two of which fell on the lockdown, I have made seven productions in London, Berlin, and Minsk, which were presented at international festivals. Our task is to discover new names and rehabilitate old ones. That's why it was very important for me to stage the play *Scattering Ravens* by Olga Prusak, a Belarusian contemporary playwright, during the protests in Minsk in 2020. This was the first turn of Belarusian theatre to the theme of NKVD repressions against the Belarusian intelligentsia. The play is based on the story of the Jewish-Belarusian poet Moisha Kulbak, who was shot by the Soviet authorities in 1937. The performance was made during the protests, the actors changed, someone was detained, and someone had to flee the country, but we managed to show it. The play is about the relationship between the poet and the authorities, with a direct reference to what was happening in Belarus at that time. After some time, our main performer was deported from the country by the authorities, and the performance itself became the last premiere in the Belarusian underground before the beginning of unprecedented repressions.

VR: What other projects are you working on that revitalize you?

VS: Now three performances are at different stages of development and reconstruction at once. The first one is a play about how we made the play *Scattering Ravens* during the protest in Minsk in 2020. It will be the stories of the actors themselves, many of them refugees now, as well as a chronicle of infamous Belarusian events and the process of making our play. I want to reassemble the original cast of that Minsk show and perform it once more, but in a safe context.

The second performance *P for Pischevsky* is a documentary court hearing about the homophobic attack in Minsk that led to the death of Mikhail Pischevsky. Andrei Zavalei, an LGBTQ activist and our general manager in Belarus, made this project possible. This performance is a coproduction of our Belarusian team with Berlin's "Cheap Theatre," which we recently presented at Berlin's leading independent venue HAU. Now I want to include in this trial the personal experiences of our unique international performers and look at the social and political realities of

Backstage Group Photo "P for Pischevsky," Hunch Theatre Archive.

Belarus and contemporary Europe through the prism of sexuality. The third performance is the personal story of my colleague Oliver Bennett, in which he tries to establish his kinship with the legendary London street actor Henry Wallace, who was arrested over five hundred times. We are now preparing a big international tour of this documentary one-man show, which was a great success in London.

Chapter 3

PERFORMING RESISTANCE VIRTUALLY: THE DIGITAL HOME OF THE FREE KUPALAUTSY

We, the actors of the Yanka Kupala Theatre, watch with pain and horror, what is happening in our country. We respect the law and human rights, but every night we live as if we are on the front lines.[…] We are against the terror and violence. We are against the bloodshed in our country.[1]

Actors of the Yanka Kupala Theatre, August 12, 2020

We do not have the opportunity to meet you today in our house, on our stage to fully celebrate this historic day. So fate determined. This is our way. The way of truth. The way of Belarus.[2]

The Free Kupalautsy, September 14, 2020

When the massive protests erupted in Belarus in August 2020, as we have seen, many cultural figures and theatre workers joined their fellow protestors—demanding change: fair elections, the release of political prisoners, and an end to the violent, oppressive rule of the regime. Kureichik, members of the Belarus Free Theatre, the Contemporary Art Theatre, the Belarusian Army Drama Theatre, and many others across Belarus looked for various

---

1 Qtd in Andriej Moskwin, "Cultural Protest in Belarus: Theatres during the Belarusian Revolution (2020)." *Canadian Slavonic Papers* 63, nos. 3–4 (2022): 358–370, 363.
2 First video posting of the collective of artists who resigned from the Yanka Kupala National Academic Theatre in August 2020 in solidarity with the mass protestors. The video is from a selection of the popular play *Simon the Musician* by Yakob Kolas presented to mark the centenary of the Theatre. https://www.youtube.com/@kupalaucyhttps://www.youtube.com/watch?v=pS_Kusbx_5g.

ways to express their opposition.[3] Members of the elite, state-funded Yanka Kupala National Academic Theatre in Minsk also showed solidarity with the protesters, in spite of strict policies against political activity in their employment contracts and a decades-long culture of self-censorship.[4] Like so many of their counterparts, most of the company members who stood up against the regime ended up in exile. Their stature could not shield them from the regime's reckless reaction to the growing opposition and near-total shutdown of civil society, independent media, and the arts. In spite of the loss of their jobs, their stage, and eventually their homes, members of the Kupala reformed as the "Free Kupalautsy," using the digital space as their new creative home. Over the next few years, the company members who left the theatre regrouped, reclaiming their identity as "the national theatre" and found new ways to form a community, promote Belarusian culture and language, agitate for political prisoners, remember, and mourn. Although most of their productions have been adaptations rather than documentary or verbatim plays, by depicting the act of filming, the use of parallel texts and everyday actions like letter writing, and the use of costumes and props to signal the representation of contemporary events in Belarus acted in a similar manner. This chapter focuses primarily on the first season of the free Kupalautsy, which defiantly met underground to record performances it made available virtually and found a surprisingly supportive and engaged audience.

By mid-August 2020, as the security forces became increasingly violent and the number of detentions grew, members of the Yanka Kupala National Academic Theatre, along with the managing director and former Minister of Culture, Pavel Latushka, and Artistic Director Mikalai Pinihin, spoke out, using their elite status to draw exposure. On August 13, the theatre company made several written demands to the Ministry of Culture, including the release of political prisoners, an investigation of abuse of protestors, and an end to the spreading of "false information on state television," and new, fair elections.[5] As Andreij Moskwin has described, Latushka and company members began expressing opposition more boldly and participating in demonstrations, eventually calling "for the resignation of the Interior Minister, Iury Karaeu, and those responsible for the brutal treatment of detainees."[6] Kureichik has written, "It came as a shock when [Latushka]

---

3 Moskwin, 362 and Andrei Kureichik, "Theatre in Belarus: We Will Never Be the same." *American Theatre Magazine*, https://www.americantheatre.org/2020/08/24/ theatre-in-belarus-we-will-never-be-the-same/.

4 Moskwin, 359.

5 Ibid., 363.

6 Ibid., 364.

came out in support of the protesters' anger. No civil servant of such a high rank has ever contradicted Lukashenko's regime."[7] Belarusian writer Viktor Martinovich said, "I liked how [Mikalai] Pinihin [...] conducted himself- that was a discovery. His actions and those of all the members of the Kupala deserve respect."[8] There was a general feeling that such visible opposition by a civil servant like Latushka, along with leading cultural figures such as Noble Prize-winning author Sviatlana Aleksievich and popular writers and favored performers, alongside the massive protests, would pressure the regime to capitulate. Instead, on August 17, Latushka was fired by Iury Bondar, the Minister of Culture, who controlled all administrative appointments at cultural institutions across the country. Nearly all members of the theatre's troupe, including Pinihin, left the theatre in protest on August 19, 2020.[9]

In September, this group, reforming itself as the free, or independent, Kupalautsy recorded a video with members of the troupe taking individual lines and uploaded it on the YouTube channel that would become their creative home:

The Kupalautsy Theatre is the company and staff of the Yanka Kupala National Academic Theatre. On 14 September 1920, the Belarusian State Theatre started working in the building of the Minsk City Theatre. In 1944, it was named after the great Belarusian poet and playwright, Yanka Kupala. We had our share of trials and joyful moments during this turbulent century, and in 2020 we were preparing to celebrate our centenary. Yet things turned out differently: on 26 August we left the theatre in solidarity with the Belarusian nation that had taken to the streets in peaceful protests against the violence and lawlessness that had swept the country. We are a national theatre because we have been standing by our nation for all these years. Now we are the free Kupalautsy Theatre. We have left our home, but we are sure we will come back to it. Our page is about our return, our long way home.

It is significant that the group claimed "Kupalautsy" as its name. Rather than seeing their work as a break from the past, members viewed their work

---

7 Kureichik, https://www.americantheatre.org/2020/08/24/theatre-in-belarus-we-will-never-be-the-same/.

8 Serge Sakarau, "'Nowadays I Often Cry': An Interview with Victor Martinovich." *Europzine*, February 2, 2021, https://www.eurozine.com/nowadays-i-often-cry/.

9 "Artisty belorusskogo Kupalovskogo teatra uvolilic' vsled za Latushko," August 19, 2020, *Gazeta.ru*, https://www.gazeta.ru/culture/news/2020/08/19/n_14817559.shtml.

as a continuation of the work of Yanka Kupala and the theatre that claimed his name amidst the so-called Great Patriotic War. Kupala (1882–1942), born Ivan Lutsevich, is one of Belarus's most esteemed literary figures, notable especially as a poet and playwright who wrote in Belarusian (which was banned when he first began writing in the language) and brought awareness of a distinctive Belarusian culture to Europe and Russia. Kupala was a Romantic poet who celebrated Belarusian folk culture, land, and language and strongly encouraged Belarusian independence. Kupala's vision, the Belarusian government archives note, was "marked by democratism, anti-violence, and assertion of humanistic spiritual values."[10] A victim of Stalinist repressions, he navigated the system for many years until he died mysteriously falling down a staircase in Moscow in 1942. Kupala remained a symbol of resistance and Belarusian revival.

Because independent theatres were banned in Belarus following the 2020 elections, the Kupalautsy could not hold performances for a live audience, so the collective moved into a digital space, not yet controlled by the regime in mid-September. Some of the plays produced were mounted and recorded on stages, while others were filmed in homes and non-theatrical spaces. In an interview in June 2022, actress Krystsina Drobysh described her fear and uncertainty of doing this work in Belarus in fall 2020 and spring 2021, meeting secretively to plan and record performances. Eventually, it became too dangerous to get the company together in the country.[11] Many members emigrated to Poland and continued this work, trying to hold together a Belarusian community in exile while producing virtual work for audiences at home. Over time, their productions have become more experimental, the traditional theatrical hierarchies have dissolved, and the digital space has remained activated, even after members of the group began to perform live.

From September 2020 to June 2021, the Kupalautsy produced a steady stream of short films and filmed theatrical productions for 144,000 YouTube subscribers. These digital works, produced during the uncertain first year following the elections, inspired solidarity and built community through memory; critiqued authoritarianism and complicit State actors through metaphor; represented intergenerational conflict; preserved Belarusian culture, language, and traditions; and provided space for collective mourning. Belarusian theatre critic Denis Martinovich noted that the popularity of

---

10 http://archives.gov.by/en/welcome-to-the-archives-of-belarus-website/subject-guides-to-archival-records/famous-people/yanka-kupala-personality-and-work.

11 "Z trupy 'Kupalautsau' sykhodzits'adna z galounykh zorak," *Zerkalo*, June 27, 2022, https://zerkalo42.global.ssl.fastly.net/news_/cellar/16047.html?f&fbclid=IwAR0Nb QsLSp055EX2uqD2JdCiFp0A-BoiBd-NKoZFCOfqAp3P8BaDM0rurKs.

the Kupalautsy YouTube channel, with over 100,000 views per event in 2021, might revive interest in theatre-going in Belarus, which had been lagging in recent years.[12]

Founded on September 14, 1920, as the Belarusian State Theatre at the Minsk City Theatre, according to its official history, the Yanka Kupala Theatre, as it was renamed in 1944, became the leading company and actor training school in Belarus. Throughout its history, it was granted special government recognition, receiving the status of "Academic" in 1955 and "National" in 1993.[13] Highly lauded director Mikalai Pinihin, who had been working at the Tovstonogov Bolshoi Drama Theatre in Moscow, returned to Minsk to become the Artistic Director of the theatre in 2009. Pinihin had established his reputation as an innovative, contemporary director in the late 1980s and early 1990s at the Yanka Kupala National Theatre before moving to work in Moscow. According to Moskwin, a leading scholar on Belarusian theatre, Pinihin transformed the theatre as an artistic director, working to revitalize the repertoire and the company's approach to the classics in order to develop Belarusian culture and identity for a contemporary audience.[14] As managing director, Pavel Latushka, former Minister of Culture and Ambassador to France, supported this renewal. The departure of Latushka, Pinihin, and most of the acting company in 2020, along with the tightening censorship, assured a return to stagnation and a lackluster repertoire.

The Locals by Yanka Kupala

The first full-length work produced by the independent Kupalautsy was *The Locals* by Yanka Kupala, originally staged by Pinihin at the National Theatre in 1990, where it remained for nearly 20 years in the repertoire. The play is a satire set in the period between 1918 and 1920, following a brief period of independence, when Belarus was contested as a Polish or Russian territory by the two embattled nations. Through the central character of Mikita Znosak, who attempts to adapt to whichever regime is in power at the moment, the play critiques Belarusians who deny their own language and heritage and quickly subordinate themselves. The play celebrates the teacher, Yanka Zolnik, an idealist who cherished Belarusians' distinctive

---

12 Tatiana Nevedomskaya, "Teatr i protest v Belarusi," *DW*, August 08, 2021, https://www.dw.com/ru/teatr-i-protest-v-belarusi-chto-s-kupalovskim-i-byvshimi-ego-akterami/a-58930956?maca=rus-tco-dw.

13 Yanka Kupala National Academic Theatre Website, https://kupalauski.by/teatr/history/.

14 Moskwin, 361.

culture and dreams of an Independent Belarus, though neither he nor Znosak ultimately survived the Red Army. Pinihin had been preparing a new version of the play for the Yanka Kupala National Academic Theatre's centenary on September 14, 2020, before most of the company resigned. Instead of opening the play in their theatre, the members regrouped to premiere the play on their YouTube channel on October 12, 2020. By presenting the work digitally as the Kupalautsy, the newly formed collective in essence took the identity of the theatre with them and claimed itself as the true national theatre.

Kupala wrote the work in 1922, and the Yanka Kupala National Academic Theatre's predecessor, Belarusian State Theatre-1, attempted to stage the play, even making edits to avoid censorship. Following its first performance, however, authorities removed it from the stage and even banned the written version.[15] The director Valery Masluk tried to stage the play again in 1982, the centenary of Yanka Kupala's birth, at the Mahilou Drama Theatre, but once again, the production was prohibited. That same year, a publication of the play was forbidden.[16] It wasn't until Mikalai Pinihin staged the play in 1990 at the Yanka Kupala Academic Theatre that the play became part of the national repertoire. Pinihin's production was celebrated for its innovative blend of puppet, folk, and contemporary performance styles, becoming what critic Dzianis Marsinovich called a "symbol of the epoch."[17]

The free Kupalautsy's October 2020 YouTube revival, directed by Pinihin, was filmed in an exposed theatre interior with only a few basic structures, metal folding chairs and costumes suggestive of early twentieth-century rural Belarus. The production disrupted the play's actions to highlight the filming process and the act of making performance. The very process of producing the play was a defiant and celebratory act. In its celebration and invocation of Kupala, the collective aligned itself with the revival of a civic nationalism that had been growing in resistance to Russian cultural and economic colonization and Lukashenka's movement toward a union state between Russia and Belarus. Members of the theatre sought to reawaken distinctive Belarusian cultural and linguistic practices, which were essentially banned by Lukashenka's regime following the 2020 elections. The troupe did as Latushka had recommended before leaving the country, "The most important thing is that you survive and continue working [...], using the Belarusian language, introducing Belarusian and international

---

15 Dzianis Marcinovic, "The Locals Play as a Symbol of the Epoch, *Ziernie-Performa*," April 5, 2015, http://en.ziernie-performa.net/2015/04/05/the-locals-play-as-a-symbol-of-the-epoch/.

16 Ibid.

17 Ibid.

plays to the stage, and performing the wonderful productions of Mikalai Pinihin [...]"[18] The digital production, Moskwin noted, "met with euphoria" and broke "viewing records."[19]

In early spring 2021, the group produced a series of short film recitations of poems by Yanka Kupala. In each, a single actor appears in their home, writing Kupala's poem as a letter for political prisoners, a mobilizing act of solidarity urged often by Tsikhanouskaya. In a country where all visible acts of solidary with the opposition were dangerous, this series of short films, reviving the revolutionary spirit of Kupala and drawing on prohibited white–red–white symbolism, sought to preserve the spirit of the August 2020 protests and encourage a level of action a frightened and brutalized citizenry could still enact. Ales Malchanau and Raman Padaliaka were among those to record video poems in Belarusian for the series. The poems included "Spring Is Yet to Come" (1908), "For Our Own Freedom" (1911), and "Be Brave" (1913). The poems aligned well with the opposition movement that had lost its initial momentum as so many activists were imprisoned or exiled and, using Kupala's example, their recitations enacted hope, courage, and endurance.

Fear: Parts I, II, and III after Bertolt Brecht

Shortly after the appearance of poems invoking the early twentieth-century fight for Belarusian independence, the Kupalautsy shifted to another fraught, resonant historical parallel. The company streamed the trilogy *Fear: Parts I, II*, and *III* from March 27 to 30, 2021. The troupe released Part I on World Theatre Day, March 27. The streaming also aligned with the thwarted Freedom Day protests and celebrations planned by opposition leaders to begin on March 25, 2021, in an effort to rebuild momentum for the opposition movement. Over 100 people in Belarus were arrested for participating in the small in-person protests, recording or photographing events of the day, or simply being on the street during this time.[20] Although there were solidarity marches in cities throughout Eastern Europe on Freedom Day, Tsikhanouskaya's hopes for large demonstrations in Belarus were derailed by the strong military presence and rumors of government plans to stage a terrorist attack as a false flag operation to excuse excessive force against protestors. In spite of the absence of massive demonstrations,

---

18 Moskwin, 364.
19 Ibid., 366.
20 "Police Detain Over 100, Including Media Editors," *Reuters*, March 27, 2021, https://www.reuters.com/article/us-belarus-election-protests/belarus-police-detain-over-100-including-opposition-media-editors-idUSKBN2BJ0BE.

dissent was registered through symbolic actions such as firework displays, the appearance of white–red–white flags on buildings, and virtual solidarity events such as the Kupalautsy production of *Fear*.

Brecht's play, *Fear and Misery of the Third Reich*, which he wrote in exile in 1938, served as a clear opposition play for the Kupalautsy. The anti-Lukashenka opposition long made use of references to World War II and fascism in its fight against the regime. Brecht's play, a series of 18 vignettes, depicts the way the Nazis used coercion and violence to overtake the military, judiciary, media, religious institutions, and labor unions, creating confusion, fear, and complicity in public and domestic life. The Kupalautsy reordered and removed many scenes, but the company kept the central scenes depicting the complicity of the Judiciary; a Nazi's visit to his girlfriend and suspicion of her brother's involvement in the resistance; a jailer's torture of an inmate whom he blames for his own physical exhaustion while beating him; the Jewish wife packing to leave her husband in order to protect him; and parents worrying that their son will inform on them. The production, filmed with minimal furniture and properties on a fully white stage and virtual background, made the world appear to exist in a dream. The void in which the play's action took place highlighted the stagelessness and theatrical exile of this company of players, "a theatre without a stage."[21]

Historically suggestive costumes signified the German late 1930s, but the resonance in the stories and the familiarity of the actors brought the production unquestionably into the present. In many ways, the production invoked a call to resistance that paralleled the official Belarusian Victory narrative of the Great Patriotic War that centralizes the Belarusian opposition as crucial to the final defeat of the Nazis. An estimated 2.3–2.4 million Belarusians died during the German three-year occupation, but "the pride of victory over Nazi Germany came to form the basis of collective memory."[22] Endurance and unwillingness to accept defeat would be signaled through the performance. While the play also offered an opportunity to mourn great losses and express the victimization of Belarusians, it can also be viewed as a condemnation of the State actors who sustain a brutal regime and a call to action and solidarity against repressions. Members of the opposition in

---

21 Advertising on the Kupalautsy YouTube, Instagram, and Facebook pages for the production, March 2020.

22 Per Anders Rudling, "'Unhappy Is the Person Who Has No Motherland:' National Ideology and History Writing in Lukashenka's Belarus," in *War and Memory in Russia, Ukraine, and Belarus*, ed. Julie Fedor, Markku Kangaspuro, Jussi Lassila, and Tatiana Zhurzhenko (Basingstoke: Palgrave-Macmillan, 2017), 74–75.

2020–2021 often invoked parallels between Lukashenka's crackdown and Nazism and tried to upend the regime's narratives that the 2020 protestors were terrorists, foreign agents, and subhuman disposables. The performance of *Fear* combated the State's narrative and echoed scenes viewers had recently watched on Telegram channels, depicting the regime's brutality.

Woyzeck after Georg Büchner

In one of its most heart-wrenching productions, the Kupalautsy streamed a contemporary adaptation of Georg Büchner's *Woyzeck* directed by Raman Padaliaka on April 2, 2021. The highly stylized production created a nightmare of terror and violence. Büchner's *Woyzeck*, written in the 1830s and unfinished when the author died in 1837, is loosely based on the historical case of a jealous barber who stabbed his mistress to death in a rageful fit in 1821 and was condemned to death. The play develops through 25 clipped episodes in which the struggling, working-class Woyzeck encounters various archetypal forms of authority: economic, judicial, military, and medical. His physical and mental health deteriorate due to his exploitation, and his jealousy and suspicion of his love and mother of his child, Marie, grows. Radical both in its political expression and form, the play helped shape European modernism in the theatre and has been an engine for stage experimentation for over a century.

In Padaliaka's production, Woyzeck is so degraded and brutalized by his superiors and doctors that he becomes part of the violent system of oppression in his attack on the nightclub singer and his lover, Marie, portrayed by four different actresses. Padaliaka's *Woyzeck* depicts a world in which there is no resistance or hope, only the horror of violence, rape, and murder. The bleak nightmare is staged on a spare black stage with only a simple white bench with two red pillows and a screen behind for projections. Two actors, as doctors, wear white aprons, tall, cylindrical caps, and long red rubber gloves for carving into Woyzeck and the pregnant Marie. The other male actors wear all black pants, boots, caps, and long shirts reminiscent of the Belarusian OMON riot police. The women wear identical black sequence dresses, long red tights, gloves, boots, and bright red lipstick, which Woyzeck, now covered in a black balaclava, uses to mark their murder as he transforms into an instrument of the State. In this world, everyone is a prisoner and under the control of the State. The production was eerily prescient of the arrest of Raman Pratasevich, the journalist and primary editor of the Nexta Telegram channel, who was taken into custody when his Ryanair flight to Lithuania was forced to land in Belarus due to fraudulent bomb-threat claims in May 2021. Tortured and terrorized by the state, Pratasevich was forced under duress into false statements in support of Lukashenka and his regime.[23]

Ongoing Work as a "National" Theatre

The Kupalautsy continued to produce digital theatre performances until its first official season closed in June 2021. Reclaiming its heritage, the group presented the musical comedy *Paulinka* by Yanka Kupala, an annual favorite of the Yanka Kupala National Academic Theatre, as well as a contemporary Polish play, *Gardenia*, by Elzbieta Chowaniac, about four generations of strained mother–daughter relations. These two productions reveal the poles of the collective as it has charted its path following the troupe's departure from the Yanka Kupala National Academic Theatre. It maintains Pinihin's approach to developing the repertoire at the theatre, where he introduced contemporary European dramaturgy, contemporary adaptations, and heritage works as a means of growing Belarusian theatrical experimentation while preserving its language and culture.[24] *Gardenia* presses the collective further into contemporary works and experimental production methods, while the production of *Paulinka* reveals the troupe's assertion of its place as a national theatre.

After most of its members left the State Theatre in August 2020, the first play performed at the official Kupala National Academic Theatre by the remaining 20 actors along with new student recruits was *Paulinka*, and Lukashenka himself attended a rehearsal noting, "the real blood of the theatre was renewed" after the resignation of its leading players.[25] The production and the teary-eyed, melodramatic support of its new artistic director Olga Nefedova for Lukashenka has been disparaged by members of the opposition as laughable. Staging its own popular version of the play, the free Kupalautsy contested any statement about the true nature or "real blood" of the theatre being with those who remained in the building. The Kupalautsy members claimed their lineage to Yanka Kupala and remained driven to promote their beloved playwright's principles in celebration of the Belarusian language, culture, and independence.

23 Steven Butler, "Why Authoritarian Governments Force Journalists Like Belarus's Raman Pratasevich into Public Confessions," Committee to Protect Journalists, June 15, 2021, https://cpj.org/2021/06/why-authoritarian-governments-force-journalists-like-belaruss-raman-pratasevich-into-public-confessions/.

24 Moskwin, 361.

25 Tatiana Nevedomskaya, "Teatr i protest v Belarusi," *DW*, August 20, 2021, https://www.dw.com/ru/teatr-i-protest-v-belarusi-chto-s-kupalovskim-i-byvshimi-ego-akterami/a-58930956?maca=rus-tco-dw.

In Warsaw, Poland, where many members of the troupe have emigrated, the collective continues to develop new work for live and digital performance, supported in part by the Polish Ministry of Culture and Heritage Funds. The premiere of new works in June 2023 at Inex Fest, a festival of Belarusian theatre in Warsaw, of vastly different theatrical styles and content reveals further experimentation mixed with ongoing interest in cultivating and preserving Belarusian culture. *The Comedy of Judith* by Sergei Kavalev blends biblical texts, the Book of Judith, and Beckett monologues in a harrowing tale of one woman's struggle against tyranny and her own capacity for violence. The sharply stylized production emphasized the grotesque and horrifying world of the central character. In contrast to this experimental work, the troupe performed *Whispers*, based on the 10-year oral history and photojournalism project of Sergei Lesket, who interviewed elderly Belarusian villagers who practiced "whisper" treatments, healing incantations, to cure a range of ailments. Director Raman Padaliaka worked with Lesket in developing the straightforward, documentary-style stage performance, which toured throughout Poland and Lithuania.

Members of the Kupalautsy living in exile experience ongoing precarity as the Russian war in Ukraine continues to generate unrest and uncertainty. In an interview with *Radio Svaboda* in June 2023, one of the leading actresses of the theatre, Valentina Hartsuyeva talked about her divided life, the one she lived before 2020, and the one following the elections, leaving the official theatre in Minsk and emigrating to Poland. Hartsuyeva, a film and stage actor and descendant of four generations of celebrated Belarusian performers and directors, immediately joined the Yanka Kupala National Academic Theatre upon graduation from the Belarusian State Academy of Arts in 2007. An acclaimed performer, she played such roles as Nina Zarechnaya in Chekhov's *The Seagull* and Regan in *King Lear*, in the theatre's repertoire. Before 2020, everything in her life was predictable, she said, and "transparent to me. Maybe not very interesting, not very colorful."[26]

In December 2021, having been blacklisted in Belarus, she returned to Kyiv for several months to film a television series, leaving for a tour of *Fear* with the Kupalautsy in Germany just before Russia invaded Ukraine. She understood that she couldn't go back to Ukraine or return to Belarus. She then emigrated to Poland, where she faced uncertainty and worries about financial security, but she also appreciated the expressive freedom she found

---

26 "Gistorya Kupalauskaga skonchylacya na 100-godz'dzi," *Radio Svaboda*, June 05, 2023, https://www.svaboda.org/a/32445131.html?fbclid=IwAR1PilxO4ZeNqZsRx YI4Ymvg26MOqYgAwlp7J5nP9K_DOwbIjxozqprAJPg.

and opportunities to generate ideas for the collective, which wouldn't have been possible in her position in Minsk. In 2023, she continued to perform with the collective in Poland and on tour, which she characterized as giving her and the others a sense of purpose and community along with a way to support those still living in Belarus under the restrictive regime. Staying active with the work of the theatre has helped her survive and stay focused, but she expressed that she had not really had the opportunity to grieve all that she had lost.

In the interview, Hartsuyeva noted that she believes she will return to Belarus one day and perform again on the Kupala stage. When asked what she'd like to perform, she answered, *Paulinka*. For Drobysh, who began working on a project in 2022 recording children's books in Belarusian, continuing to develop and cultivate the Belarusian community and culture in exile remains essential, even as she moved away from stage performances. "The main goal," she has said, "is to stay Belarusian."[27]

For two years, the free Kupalautsy allowed these exiled theatre artists to remain in the community, find purpose, and continue their profession as one crisis after another destabilized their world. The work they produced captured the anxiety and precarity in the aftermath of the 2020 election while signaling a refusal to be disposable, as the Belarusian regime attempts to make its opponents. Although dispossessed, the members of the company reclaimed their heritage and status as the national theatre through their performances, refusing to comply, to be invisible, or to forget.

---

27 Zerkalo, "Z Trupy 'Kupalautsau."

TOWARD A CONCLUSION

On October 30, 2023, Kupalautsy actress Krystsina Drobysh posted photos on her social media accounts of a forgotten production that had taken place in 1991 and was subsequently removed from public records. The photos are of an adaptation of Nobel Prize-winning Belarusian author Sviatlana Aleksievich's oral history, *Zinky Boys: Soviet Voices from the Afghanistan War*, at the Yanka Kupala National Theatre in Minsk, Belarus. Due to controversy around the production, which was televised in 1992, and a lawsuit against Aleksievich by mothers who objected to the dark portrayal of their soldier sons, the production was removed from the stage and most records of it disappeared. Due to her own sleuthing and contacts, Drobysh recovered documents and memories of the production, directed by Valery Raevsky, with a cast that included most of the troupe at the time. Drobysh told Kamunikat.org, the Belarusian Internet Library, why she wanted to recuperate the historical event:

> Not only the play itself, but also the fact of its existence was erased from history. In approximately the same way, the dismissal of nearly the entire troupe of the Kupala Theatre in 2020 could have been erased from memory, if it had not happened in the age of the internet. That's why it was extremely important for me to restore this gap.[1]

Following the impulse of Belarusian theatre artists to document their experiences and work in 2020, the book aims foremost to create a public record of the performances of these artists in a time of crisis. Through historical description and dramaturgical analysis, photographs, and a vital interview with a key figure, this account attempts to capture various forms of preservation.

---

1 "Yak sudzili Sviatlana Aleksievich," Kamunikat.org, October 17, 2023, https://kamunikat.org/yak-sudzili-svyatlanu-aleksiyevich?fbclid=IwAR2LUVfgu1xFHtAA SieTty24mHX_A7h2iSjZX84hHICORxLZeSG_keOIH5s.

As we have seen, Belarusian theatre artists were key players in the resistance movement in Belarus, helping to mobilize the resistance, bringing international attention to the crisis, shaping counternarratives to the regime's propaganda, and providing spaces—both digital and physical—to mourn and grieve those who were murdered or forced into exile. Documentary theatre, film, and digital performance became a substantial way to respond to the crisis, building on historical evidence, phenomenological detail, and lived experience. While cultural objects like theatrical performance and film are often relegated to a secondary dimension to journalism, human rights activism, and legal practices in times of humanitarian crises, it is clear here that the realm of the arts has been vital throughout the campaign to disrupt Lukashenka's stronghold on power and public opinion. The work of these artists, especially the Kupalautsy, to capture and promote a sense of national identity through the use of Belarusian language and reclamation of Belarusian writers and historical symbols continues in spite of their exile.

Although it may seem evident that the Belarusian resistance movement failed yet again in 2020, many argue that the vast mobilization and resistance to Lukashenka's regime has had enduring affects and created fractures in the dictator's "social contract of basic economic well-being and political stability" along with a growing sense of national identity.[2] The protestors failed to oust Lukashenka in the immediate aftermath of the fraudulent election due to the severe repressions and sustained violence, Lukashenka's deep stronghold on the economy and security forces, and lack of a clear, cohesive, and durable countermovement. Nevertheless, recent analyses suggest a weakening of faith in institutions, increased polarization on geopolitical issues and type of media consumption, and a growing sense of a national identity through language, symbols, and shared history, and desire for Belarusian sovereignty.

Lukashenka attempted to consolidate his power through a constitutional plebiscite on February 27, 2022, just days after Russia invaded Ukraine from Belarusian as well as Russian territory. Like most direct votes and elections in authoritarian regimes, Fabian Burkhardt and Jan Matti Dollbaum point out that the main purposes of such events are to "maintain a façade of democratic process while demonstrating the continued strength of the regime to domestic and foreign audiences."[3] For Lukashenka, this vote

---

2 Olga Onuch and Gwendolyn Sasse, "The Dynamics of Mass Mobilization in Belarus," *Nationalities Papers* 51.4 (2023): 736–743.

3 Fabian Burkharddt and Jan Matti Dollbaum, "Lukashenka's Constitutional Plebescite and the Polarization of Belarusian Society," *Communist and Post-Communist Studies*, 56.3 (2023): 98–126.

finally settled any questions contesting his power and hoped to return to the status quo, as he has done in the past, but research suggests that there is ongoing social and political fragmentation and little in terms of policy holding the pro-Lukashenka support together.[4] Elena Korosteleva and Irina Petrova have argued that the social entanglements established through the protest movement endure, accounting for "a rise of Belarusian *peoplehood*" or a stronger sense of self-worth and community belonging.[5] Brought together into communities in various ways during the protests, they argue, "served as a catalyst and amplifier of hidden processes of change, making them both inevitable and irreversible, even without apparent signs of real transformation."[6] Activities of the opposition abroad, occasional small "flash mobs" of individuals in red and white, and sidewalk chalk protest art indicate the perseverance, if muffled, of the resistance. This is not yet concluded.

The theatre artists depicted throughout this book played a significant role in the transformed landscape, underground though it may be, due to their courageous performances and bodily presence in the initial stages of the movement to disempower the authoritarian regime. While members of the Belarus Free Theatre reiterated this bodily enactment of resistance, the 2020 movement drew newly activated performers and dramatists to take a stand. Thwarted in a devastating way in their stance, the theatre artists who joined the protests searched for new ways to stay engaged and mobilize their audiences. Kureichik, who helped shape the performances of the opposition leaders in the lead-up to the election, launched a global campaign for international recognition and response to the regime's crackdown. Converting traumatic experiences into creative action, his plays denounce the regime and reclaim the voices of its victims. The Belarus Free Theatre, Aliaksei Paluyan, and the Free Kupalautsy flooded the social media airwaves with a refusal of disposability and dispossession.

When the risk of bodily exposure to the violence of the regime became too much to withstand, having mobilized their vulnerability to the extreme, these artists found new ways to assemble and expose their resistance. The state denied the protestors access to public space through forcible removal, violence, and imprisonment, but these artists reclaimed and reformed spaces of assembly through the internet and social media networks. Convening on YouTube and

---

4 Ibid.; Onuch and Sasse; Elena Korosteleva and Irina Petrova, "Power, People, and the Political: Understanding the Many Crises in Belarus," *Nationalities Papers* 51.4 (2023): 875–887.

5 Elena Korosteleva and Irina Petrova, 882.

6 Ibid., 883.

Facebook as a virus continues to rage brought together thousands globally in solidarity. In spite of an unknown and unknowable future, these theatre artists, and the filmmakers who amplified them, leveraged their collective vulnerability in a refusal to submit to the regime's dominance. They've laid claim to the story, to their language, to their land, and to the grievable bodies buried there. It was, indeed, a time for theatre.

BIBLIOGRAPHY

Arcimovich, Tania. "Modern Belarusian Theatre: A Struggle for Diversity." August 9, 2012. Accessed July 20, 2023. https://artimovich.wordpress.com/2012/08/09/modern-belarusian-theatre-a-struggle-for-diversity/.

"Artisty belorusskogo Kupalovskogo teatra uvolilic' vsled za Latushko." *Gazeta.ru*, August 19, 2020, https://www.gazeta.ru/culture/news/2020/08/19/n_14817559.shtml.

Barshcheuski, Lavon. Trans. Natalia Mamul. "Raman Padaliaka's Difficult Choice." Culture.PL, Series: The Road to Freedom: Poland in Solidarity with Belarus. September 08, 2020. https://culture.pl/en/article/raman-padaliakas-difficult-choice.

Batura, Alyena. "How to Compete in Unfair Elections." *Journal of Democracy* 33, no. 4 (Oct 2022): 47–61.

Bekus, Nelly. "Echo of 1989? Protest Imaginaries and Identity Dilemmas in Belarus." *Slavic Review* 80, no. 1 (Spring 2021): 4–15.

Bekus, N. and Gabowitsch, M. "Introduction: The Sociology of Belarusian Protest." *Slavic Review* 80, no. 1 (2021): 1–3. doi:10.1017/slr.2021.27.

Belarus Free Theatre. Official Website. https://belarusfreetheatre.com/.

Birksted-Breen, Noah. "Living in the Skin of Dictatorship: An Encounter with Belarus Free Theatre." *Cultural Geographies in Practice* 30, no. 2 (2022): 485–492.

Bodrunova, Svetlana S. "Social Media and Political Dissent in Russia and Belarus: An Introduction to the Special Issue." *Social Media and Society* 7, no. 4 (Oct–Dec 2021): 1–8.

Brantley, Ben. "Political Theatre, Brought to You by the Politically Powerless," *New York Times*. Review of *Being Harold Pinter*. January 6, 2011. https://www.nytimes.com/2011/01/07/theater/reviews/07pinter.html.

———. "Theatre Banned in Belarus but the Show Goes On." *New York Times*. October 14, 2015. https://www.nytimes.com/2015/10/18/theater/banned-in-belarus-but-the-shows-go-on.html.

Brown, Bryan. "The Translation of Protest: The Worldwide Readings Project of Andrei Kureichyk's Insulted. Belarus." *New Theatre Quarterly* 39, no. 1 (2023): 1–17.

Burkhardt, Fabian and Jan Matti Dollbaum. "Lukashenka's Constitutional Plebiscite and the Polarization of Belarusian Society." *Communist and Post-Communist Studies* 56, no. 3 (2023): 98–126.

Bury, Liz. "Irina Khalip wins PEN Pinter Prize for International Writer of Courage," *The Guardian*, October 9, 2013. https://www.theguardian.com/books/2013/oct/09/irina-khalip-pen-pinter-prize-tom-stoppard.

Butler, Judith. *Notes Toward a Performative Theory of Assembly*. Cambridge, MA and London: Harvard University Press, 2015.

Casson, John W. "Living Newspaper: Theatre and Therapy." *TDR* 44, no. 2 (2000): 107–122.

Cavendish, Dominic. "Appeal of Belarusian Theatre Representatives to the World Cultural Community." http://www.criticalmuse.com/stage/appeal-of-belarusian-theatre-representatives-to-the-world-cultural-community/.

"Connection: A Short Film Starring Jude Law." Dir. Vladimir Shcherban. *The Guardian*, September 16, 2013. https://www.theguardian.com/stage/video/2013/sep/16/connection-jude-law-video.

De Castro, Colette. "Subterranean Explosion: Aliaksei Paluyan's *Courage*." *East European Film Bulletin* 116 (Summer 2021). https://eefb.org/perspectives/aliaksei-paluyans-courage-2021/.

Drama and Theatre with John Freedman. Website. https://jfreed16.wixsite.com/johnfreedman.

Fedor, Julie, Markku Kangaspuro, Jussi Lassila, and Tatiana Zhurzhenko, eds. *War and Memory in Russia, Ukraine, and Belarus*. Cham, Switzerland: Palgrave-Macmillan, 2017.

Flynn, Molly. *Witness Onstage: Documentary Theatre in Twenty-First-Century Russia*. 1st ed. Manchester, England: Manchester University Press, 2020.

Fragkou, Marissia. *Ecologies off Precarity in Twenty-First Century Theatre: Politics, Affect, Responsibility*. London and New York: Methuen Drama, 2019.

Freedman, John. "Andrei Kureichik's 'Insulted. Belarus.' One Year On." *The Theatre Times*, September 2, 2021. https://thetheatretimes.com/andrei-kureichiks-insulted-belarus-one-year-on/.

———. "Belarus and Ukraine: No Longer Hinterlands." *Critical Stages* no. 25 (June 2022). https://www.critical-stages.org/25/belarus-and-ukraine-no-longer-russias-hinterlands/.

———. "Presenting Andrei Kureichik's Insulted. Belarus. to a World in Lockdown." *Mise en Abyme* 8, no. 1 (2021): 61–78.

———. *Real and Phantom Pains: An Anthology of New Russian Drama*. Washington, DC: New Academia Press, 2014.

Friedman, Misha. *Two Women in Their Time: The Belarus Free Theatre and the Art of Resistance*. New York: The New Press, 2020.

"Gistorya Kupalauskaga skonchylacya na 100-godz'dzi," Radio Svaboda, June 05, 2023. https://www.svaboda.org/a/32445131.html?fbclid=IwAR1PilxO4ZeNqZsRxYI4Ymvg26MOqYgAw1p7J5nP9K_DOwbIjxozqprAJPg.

Insulted. Belarus. Official website. https://www.insultedbelarus.com/.

Landsberg, Torsten and Scott Roxborough, "'Courage' on the Front Lines of the Belarus Protests," *DW*, 06/11/2021. https://www.dw.com/en/courage-on-the-frontline-of-the-belarus-protests/a-57843164.

Leach, Robert. *The Revolutionary Theatre*, London and New York: Routledge, 1994.

Lewis, Simon. "'Tear Down These Prison Walls!' Verses of Defiance in the Belarusian Revolution." *Slavic Review* 80, no. 1 (Spring 2021): 15–27.

Khalezin, Nicolai. *Belarus Free Theatre Staging a Revolution: New Plays from Eastern Europe*. London: Oberon Books, 2016.

Korosteleva, Elena and Irina Petrova. "Power, People, and the Political: Understanding the Many Crises in Belarus." *Nationalities Papers* 51, no. 4 (2023): 875–887.

Kureichik, Andrei. Trans. John Freedman. "Theatre in Belarus Will Never Be the Same." *American Theatre Magazine*, August 24, 2020. https://www.americantheatre.org/2020/08/24/theatre-in-belarus-we-will-never-be-the-same/.

———. Trans. John Freedman. *Two Plays of Revolution*. Chapel Hill, NC: Laertes Press, 2023.

Manaev, Oleg, Natalie Rice, and Maureen Taylor. "The Evolution and Influence of Russian and Belarusian Propaganda during the Belarus Presidential Election and Ensuing Protests of 2020." *Canadian Slavonic Papers* 63, no. 3–4 (2022): 371–402.

Mann, Emily. *Testimonies: Four Plays*, New York: Theatre Communications Group, 1997.

Marples, David R. "Changing Belarus." *Canadian Slavonic Papers* 63 no. 3–4 (2021) 278–295.

Martin, Carol, ed. *Dramaturgy of the Real on the World Stage*, London: Palgrave Macmillan, 2010.

Moskwin, Andreij. "Cultural Protest in Belarus: Theatres during the Belarusian Revolution (2020)." *Canadian Slavonic Papers* 63, no. 3–4 (2022): 358–370.

Nevedomskaya, Tatiana. "Teatr i protest v Belarusi," *DW*, August 08, 2021. https://www.dw.com/ru/teatr-i-protest-v-belarusi-chto-s-kupalovskim-i-byvshimi-ego-akterami/a-58930956?maca=rus-tco-dw.

Nikolayenko, Olena. "'I Am Tired of Being Afraid': Emotions and Protest Participation in Belarus." *International Sociology* 37, no. 1 (2022): 78–96.

Onuch, Olga and Gwendolyn Sasse. "The Dynamics of Mass Mobilization in Belarus." *Nationalities Papers* 51, no. 4 (2023): 736–743.

Paluyan, Aliaksei, dir. *Courage*. Living Pictures Productions, 2021.

Robinson, Valleri. "Belarus Needs Our Help." *Public Seminar*, November 29, 2021. https://publicseminar.org/author/valleri/.

———. "Even in Exile, Belarus' Sviatlana Tsikhanouskaya Fights Authoritarianism." *UPI*, October 11, 2021. https://www.upi.com/Voices/2021/10/11/belarus-Sviatlana-Tsikhanouskaya-Belarus-election/5201633953273/.

Rohter, Larry. "Theatre Group in Belarus Is Forced Underground." *New York Times*, December 21, 2010. https://www.nytimes.com/2010/12/22/theater/22radar.html.

Rudling, Per Anders. "'Unhappy Is the Person Who Has No Motherland:' National Ideology and History Writing in Lukashenka's Belarus." War and Memory in Russia, Ukraine, and Belarus, ed. Julie Fedor, Markku Kangaspuro, Jussi Lassila, Tatiana Zhurzhenko. Cham, Switzerland: Palgrave-Macmillan (2017): 71–106.

Sakarau, Serge. "'Nowadays I Often Cry': An Interview with Victor Martinovich." *Europzine*, February 2, 2021. https://www.eurozine.com/nowadays-i-often-cry/.

Salwa, Ola. "Aliaksei Paluyan and Jörn Möllenkamp, Director and Producer of Courage," *Cineuropa*, 03/17/2021. https://cineuropa.org/en/interview/398912/.

Shchyttsova, Tatiana. "A Philosopher on the Streets of Belarus." *NewsNet* 60, no. 5 (October 2020): 1–4.

Sheward, David. "Being Harold Pinter," *Backstage*. Review of Being Harold Pinter. Updated August 15, 2012. https://www.backstage.com/magazine/article/harold-pinter-59457/.

Tikhanovskaya, Svetlana. "'I Was a Stay-at-Home Mom. Now I'm Leading a Revolution." *New York Times*, September 23, 2020. https://www.nytimes.com/2020/09/23/opinion/belarus-tikhanovskaya-opposition-leader.html.

Tsapkala, Veranaka, Nelly Bekus, Maryna Maskaliova, and David R. Marples. "The Campaign of the 'Fighting Women': The Belarus Election of 2020 and Its Aftermath—A Conversation with Veranika Tsapkala." *Canadian Slavonic Papers* 63, nos. 3–4 (2021): 403–421.

Vice, Sue. "Holocaust Testimony or 'Soviet Epic': Svetlana Alexievich's Polyphonic Texts." Holocaust Studies 29, no. 4 (2023): 547–565.

Vourlias, Christopher. "Filmmakers Launch Belarusian Film Academy to Give a Voice to Threatened Artists in Repressive Putin Ally." *Variety*, February 17, 2023. https://variety.com/2023/film/global/efm-belarusian-film-academy-1235526394/?fbclid=IwAR09O5iX13D9MAjNXsv3H5wfoIGDyR3xkpWOCXS2cKtApVjVT4B7aiBuBmE.

Way, Lucan and Amelie Tovan. "Why the 2020 Protests Failed to Oust Lukashenka." *Nationalities Papers* 51, no. 4 (2023): 787–802.

"Yanka Kupala: Personality and Work." Archives of Belarus. http://archives.gov.by/en/welcome-to-the-archives-of-belarus-website/subject-guides-to-archival-records/famous-people/yanka-kupala-personality-and-work.

"Z trupy 'Kupalautsau' sykhodzits'adna z galounykh zorak." *Zerkalo*, June 27, 2022. https://zerkalo42.global.ssl.fastly.net/news_/cellar/16047.html?f&fbclid=IwAR0NbQsLSp055EX2uqD2JdCiFp0A-BoiBd-NKoZFCOfqAp3P8BaDM0rurKs.

INDEX